Berlitz®
Spain

Original text by Emma Stanford
Updated by Nick Inman
Edited by Liz Clasen and Roger Williams
Series Editor: Tony Halliday

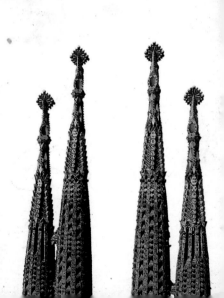

POCKET GUIDE

Spain

Third Edition (2003)
Updated 2004, 2006

PHOTOGRAPHY
AGE Fotostock 51, AKG London 20; Conor Caffrey 6, 9, 10, 13, 15, 17, 21, 26, 33, 37, 43, 51, 66, 71, 73, 77, 108, 112, 114, 117, 119, 144; Chris Coe 11, 18, 36, 42, 55, 58, 62, 64, 85, 88, 90, 95, 96, 98, 100, 103, 105, 109, 129, 133, 134, 137; Jon Davison 145; Jerry Dennis 56, 61, 78, 80, 81, 82, 143; Glyn Genin 28, 29, 35, 120; Dany Gignoux 39; Paul Murphy 70; Gary John Norman 126, 140; Mark Read 45, 46, 47, 49, 50; 54, 59, 65, 125; Neil Schlecht 40, 41; Jeroen Snijders 52; Bill Wassman 87, 92, 93, 94, 97, 107, 118, 122, 123, 130; Gregory Wrona 72, 74, 76; 110, 127, 128
Cover photograph: Jerry Dennis

CONTACTING THE EDITORS
Every effort has been made to provide accurate information in this publication, but changes are inevitable. The publisher cannot be responsible for any resulting loss, inconvenience or injury. We would appreciate it if readers would call our attention to any errors or outdated information by contacting Berlitz Publishing, PO Box 7910, London SE1 1WE, England.
Fax: (44) 20 7403 0290;
e-mail: berlitz@apaguide.co.uk
www.berlitzpublishing.com

➤ The Museo del Prado, with its art treasures, is one of the top attractions of Madrid (page 30)

Puerto Banús, one of many resorts on the Costa del Sol, is Spain's answer to St Tropez (page 81)

◄

Barcelona is home to Gaudí's eccentric Sagrada Família church (page 49)
▼

TOP TEN ATTRACTIONS

La Mezquita in Córdoba is a stunning example of Moorish architectural prowess (page 58)

With its landmark Giralda tower, Sevilla's cathedral is the world's largest Gothic church (page 55)

The futuristic Museo Guggenheim in Bilbao is the top attraction of the Basque Country (page 95)

The works of Salvador Dalí feature prominently on the Costa Brava (page 67)

The Picos de Europa provide some of the most dramatic scenery in Spain (page 86)

The Alhambra in Granada is the grandest of all monuments left by the Moors (page 60)

Spectacularly situated on the River Tajo, Toledo is famous for its cathedral and the works of El Greco (page 33)

CONTENTS

Fact Sheets

SPAIN AND ITS PEOPLE

Spain is located in the far southwest of Europe and comprises the largest part of the Iberian Peninsula (with Portugal claiming a narrow strip hugging most of the western coastline). The Balearic Islands of Ibiza, Mallorca and Menorca, in the western Mediterranean, also belong to Spain, as do the subtropical Canary Islands, off the west coast of Africa.

Evolution of Modern Spain

Starting with the Phoenicians' founding of Cádiz in 1100BC, Spain was colonised over a period of some 2,500 years by such diverse cultures as the Carthaginians, Romans, Vandals, Visigoths and the Moors, all of whom contributed something to the character of the country. It was not until the Catholic Monarchs, Fernando (Ferdinand) and Isabel, drove the last remaining Moors from their capital in Granada in 1492 that Spain became a united country. At the same time, the previously harmonious relationship between Catholics and people of Jewish and Moorish origin was broken by the Spanish Inquisition, which persecuted the latter two groups and expelled them from the country. The same year saw the event that started Spain's Golden Age – the first modern European voyage to America led to Spain becoming fabulously wealthy from her Southern American colonies. These treasures, however, were soon squandered in pointless wars and Spain retreated, introspectively, behind the formidable barrier of the great Pyrenees mountain range.

It was a desperately poor Spain that re-emerged onto the international stage in 1936, torn asunder in a violent, murderous civil war between the left-leaning Republicans – assisted by

Windmills and castles at Consuegra, central Spain

the famed International Brigades – and the right-wing Nationalists led by General Franco, helped by German and Italian military might. After his victory in 1939, Franco instituted a harsh dictatorship that ended only with his death in 1975. He was succeeded as head of state by King Juan Carlos I who, despite having been groomed as a successor by Franco, surprised the country by immediately setting in motion a rapid and bloodless transformation of Spain into a democratic constitutional monarchy. Since then, general elections have seen the government controlled by parties of both the left and of the right. During the past two decades, more and more power has devolved to the 17 autonomous regions.

Rich Scenic Diversity

Impressive mountain ranges, such as the Pyrenees and Sierra Nevada, as well as numerous lesser-known massifs, are spread throughout Spain's mainland, a large part of which forms the central plateau, or *meseta*. And, not to be outdone, the Canary Island of Tenerife has Mt Teide – the highest mountain in the country. Along Spain's Atlantic and Mediterranean coasts – and, of course, on the islands – you find almost every conceivable type of beach environment. Inland are powerful rivers, arid plateaux, wide plains and even, in Almería and on the island of Fuerteventura, desert.

While Spain is (at 504,880 sq km/ 194,885 sq miles) the third largest country in Europe, after Russia and France, it has a proportionately small population (just over 41 million). Consequently, and unusually in Europe, vast areas of the country remain wild, rugged and under-populated.

Regional Pride

Spain's varied terrain and the assimilation of so many diverse cultures have shaped the character of its peoples.

And it is, in reality, peoples in the plural. Some of the country's 17 autonomous regions are fiercely independent – both in their thinking and in their relative freedom from interference by central government, a combination that has given rise to passionate 'regional nationalism', most notably among the Catalans and Basques, but in other regions as well. This is reflected most obviously for visitors in the use of local languages rather than Castilian Spanish. In fact, only about 60 percent of Spaniards use Castilian as their natural language.

Costume reinforces regional identity – here in Murcia

Even though the regions differ widely in custom and character, they generally share a very 'Spanish' lifestyle. This includes a love of children, devotion to family and friends, and an open and inclusive social life that involves partaking of much fine food and wine. Generally, Spaniards are a garrulous, happy and contented people who place much importance in politeness, both with each other and strangers.

A Wealth of Attractions

The variety of scenery and attractions in Spain promises that there will be something of interest here to the newcomer or the seasoned traveller, and everyone in between. First-time

Modernisme in Barcelona

visitors may want to plan an itinerary that takes in the most important cities of historical interest that appeal to their particular interests.

Madrid is the Spanish capital and transport hub, located at the geographical heart of the country, and is the most obvious place to start. Not only is it of importance in its own right, but it can also be used as a base to visit a host of fascinating nearby cities and places of interest. **Barcelona**, world famous for its architecture and style, should be high on everyone's list of priorities. In fact, if anything, it has more individual attractions than Madrid. **Andalucía**, a name that is evocative of passionate emotion, is a must, with its famous white villages and spectacular Moorish heritage in the cities of **Sevilla**, **Córdoba** and **Granada**.

Many millions of people visit Spain each year with the aim of simply relaxing on a beach, and for this they have numerous options. The world-renowned **Costas** stretch from the Costa Brava at the eastern end of the Pyrenees all the way round past Gibraltar to the Costa de la Luz and the border with Portugal. Less well known is the **Costa Verde** (Green Coast), which is quite different in almost all respects from the other Costas, and stretches along the northern coast, passing through Cantabria, Asturias and Galicia on its way from the Basque Country. Don't forget, either, the **Balearic Islands** off Spain's eastern Mediterranean coast, with resorts that range from the rowdy to the refined. Visitors from the northern hemisphere in search of serious winter sunshine and swimming need look no further than the volcanic **Canary Islands**. Just off the coast of Northwest Africa, these seven islands are as different from each other as it is possible to be.

Spain also has scores of places that far fewer visitors get to see. The **Basque Country**, an entity unto itself, is graced by the elegant town of **San Sebastián** and by the stylish city of **Bilbao**, home since 1999 to the Guggenheim Museum. Ancient **Castilla y León** has the fine old Castilian cities of **Burgos**, **León**, **Salamanca** and **Segovia**. **Navarra** is renowned for the bull-running that forms part of the San Fermín Festival in **Pamplona**, but also has beautiful green countryside. **La Rioja** is justly famous for its wines, and the old kingdom of **Aragón** stretches from the high Pyrenees down to its capital **Zaragoza** and on to **Teruel**. Between Madrid and Andalucía are two of the least-visited regions of Spain: **Castilla-La Mancha**, to the east and south, is well known for its wines and Don Quixote windmills; and the isolated city of **Cuenca** is famous for its Casas Colgadas (Hanging Houses). **Extremadura** has always been remote, but that didn't stop the Romans from making **Mérida** one of its major towns. **Cáceres**, also founded by the Romans, is important for its collection of 16th-century palaces.

Modernity in Bilbao

A BRIEF HISTORY

Spain's history is as rugged and colourful as the land itself. It is a tale of Roman and Moorish domination and a glorious Golden Age; of empires and colonies conquered and defeated; of brave knights and foolish kings; and of a bloody and destructive civil war that saw Spain cut off from the international community for some four decades of the 20th century. Since Franco's death in 1975, Spain's transformation into a modern European state has been nothing short of spectacular.

Early Influences

The earliest inhabitants of the Iberian Peninsula were Paleolithic people who probably arrived via a land bridge linking Europe and Africa between Gibraltar and Morocco. As the Ice Age gripped Europe, the first Iberians put on bearskin coats, stoked up their fires, and fed off deer, bison and wild horses – just like those depicted on the walls and ceilings of caves discovered in Cantabria, near Altamira, which date back at least 15,000 years.

During the Bronze Age, Celtic migrants settled in northern and central Spain, while the south and east were inhabited by various Iberian tribes of North African origin. The Iberians had their own written language, sophisticated industry and tools, and they created fine works of art, such as the stone sculpture of a female deity, known as *La Dama de Elche* (The Lady of Elche), a star attraction at Madrid's Archaeological Museum. The Celts and the Iberians interacted where their territories overlapped and developed a distinct Celtiberian culture. The Celtiberians soon gained fame as warriors and it is said that they invented the two-edged sword, later to become standard equipment in the Roman army, and to be used against their inventors.

Before this, Phoenicians, sailing from bases in North Africa, founded several colonies in southern Spain. The first of these, established in about 1100BC, was Gadir (present-day Cádiz). Carthage, which was itself a Phoenician colony, established an empire of its own that spread as far north into Spain as Barcelona and the island of Mallorca. The Carthaginians exploited Spain's silver and lead mines and drafted the country's young, able-bodied males into their army. Barcelona was the base from which Carthaginian forces under Hannibal set out to defeat Rome in the 3rd century BC, nearly succeeding in their objective before being defeated by the Romans in the Second Punic War. The defeat of the Carthaginians left the way open for Rome to take control of the peninsula, though it took nearly 200 years to subjugate the stubbornly resistant Celtiberians.

Mérida's Roman theatre

Spain Under the Caesars

Second only to the homeland itself, Spain was to become the most important part of the Roman Empire. In many parts of the country the stamp of Roman civilisation remains: in roads and bridges, walls and vineyards, as well as in the ruins of aqueducts and amphitheatres, palaces and villas. Three living Spanish languages are descended from

Latin: Gallego (Galician), Castilian and Catalan. Roman law forms the foundation of the Spanish legal system, and Spain gave birth to Roman emperors as memorable as Trajan and Hadrian, as well as the writers Seneca and Martial.

The Romans initially divided the peninsula into two: Hispaniae Ulterior and Hispaniae Citerior ('Farther' and 'Nearer' respectively). When later, under Augustus, it was carved into three provinces, the capital cities were established at what are now Mérida (Extremadura), Córdoba (Andalucía) and Tarragona (Catalonia). Christianity came to Spain early in the Roman period. The word may have been carried by St Paul himself – he is said to have preached both in Aragón and at Tarragona.

The Visigoths

Overstretched and increasingly corrupt, Rome watched its far-flung colonies disintegrate, and Germanic tribes, some with a deserved reputation for barbarism, hastened into the vacuum. The Vandals had little to contribute to Spanish culture. However, the Gaulish Visigoths from France did bring a certain constructive influence. Former allies of Rome, they ruled from Toledo, where they displayed their intricate arts and built opulent churches.

The 300-year regime of the Visigoths never achieved any measure of national unity, and eventually foundered on the thorny question of succession. They had introduced to Spain the commendably democratic principle of elective monarchy, but this fostered a web of intrigue and assassination as contenders attempted to secure the crown. These, as well as other problems, were often blamed on the handiest scapegoat: the industrious and successful Jews. They had fared well under the Romans and early Visigoths, but at the start of the 7th century, all non-Christians were forced either to convert to Christianity or face exile.

Enter the Moors

During AD711, an expeditionary force of around 12,000 Berber troops from North Africa sailed across the Straits of Gibraltar and poured ashore into Spain. Their expertly planned invasion was led by General Tariq ibn Ziyad (the name Gibraltar is a corruption of Gibel Tariq – Tariq's Rock). His ambition was to spread the influence of Islam.

Within just three years, the Moors had reached the Pyrenees. Their initial success was assisted by ordinary citizens attracted by promises of lower taxes and by serfs offered the chance of freedom. Spanish Jews welcomed the Moors as liberators because, initially at least, the occupation forces stipulated religious tolerance. However, conversion to Islam was later forcefully encouraged, and many Christians chose to embrace the Muslim creed.

Fusion of Moorish and Christian elements at the monastery of San Juan de Duero, Soria

> **The art of medieval Moorish artisans is preserved in today's best Spanish craft buys – ceramics, tooled leather and intricate silverwork.**

The most tangible relics of the Moorish era in Spain are today among the country's greatest tourist attractions: the exquisite palaces, gardens and mosques of Córdoba, Granada and Sevilla. Thanks to the advanced irrigation techniques imported from North Africa, crops such as rice, cotton and sugar were planted, and lush orchards of almonds, pomegranates, oranges and peaches thrived. Other Moorish innovations made possible the production of paper and glass.

The Christians Strike Back

The Moorish juggernaut that trundled north from Gibraltar in 711 met no serious resistance. It was 11 years before the fragmented defenders of Christian Spain won their first battle. Exiled to the northern territory of Asturias, the Visigothic nobles, led by Pelayo, joined with local mountain folk to strike the first blow in the long-drawn-out Reconquest of Spain. Further Christian victories would be a very long time in coming, but Pelayo's success in 722 at the Battle of Covadonga (the village is now a shrine) sparked off the desire to defeat the Moors and gave heart to a struggle that was to simmer for centuries.

In the middle of the 8th century, the Christians of Asturias, under King Alfonso I, took advantage of a rebellion by Berber troops to occupy neighbouring Galicia. Here, at Santiago de Compostela, the alleged discovery of the tomb of the apostle St James (Santiago) was to make Compostela the religious focus for Spanish Christians and a rallying point for knightly defenders of the Christian faith throughout Europe. More breathing space from Moorish pressure was won in what we now know as Catalonia. Charlemagne, King of the Franks, captured Catalonia's capital, Barcelona, and established a buffer zone here between Islamic Spain and France. Spanish Christians then seized the advantage and expanded south and west into the area between Catalonia and Asturias, which soon had so many frontier castles that it became known as Castile.

The Reconquest see-sawed on for hundreds of years, as each side gained and lost territorial advantage under a succession of leaders. Over the centuries, squabbles among the Moors resulted in alliances of convenience with the Christians, and the intermingling of the two cultures was commonplace. Christians who thrived in the Moorish regions were known as Mozarabes, and their Moorish counterparts – Muslim inhabitants of Christian enclaves – were known as Mudéjars. These two names are now attached to the two most important art styles of this period, which are a blend of both Christian and Moorish elements.

Moorish tower, Palma de Mallorca

Early in the 10th century, the Asturian capital was transferred approximately 120km (75 miles) south from Oviedo to León, a symbolic step deep into former 'infidel' territory. However the Muslims were far

Statue of El Cid in Burgos

from on the run. United under the dictator al-Mansur ('the victorious'), they reclaimed León, Barcelona and Burgos and, in a severe blow to Christian morale, sacked the town of Santiago de Compostela. The death of the charismatic al-Mansur in 1002 revived Christian hopes. In 1010, they succeeded in recapturing al-Mansur's headquarters of Córdoba, and the city of Toledo fell in 1085.

The fall of Toledo sent out shock waves to Moorish rulers elsewhere in Spain and they called for help from the Almoravids, a North African confederation of Muslim Berber tribes based in Marrakesh. Known for their military prowess, they halted the Reconquest, but in the 12th century sent for further reinforcements from the Almohad fundamentalists, who stepped up the persecution of Jews and Mozarabes. The turning point of the Reconquest is held to be the Battle of Las Navas de Tolosa in 1212. In its wake, the Christian forces regained most of Spain south to Andalucía, to the point where the final Moorish stronghold at Granada was recaptured in 1492.

A Singular Nation

Up until the 15th century, the various regional kingdoms of Spain remained resolutely independent. There were some sporadic moves towards unity, which usually involved strategic marriage contracts, and it was one such royal marriage that united the shrewd Fernando of Aragón and strongly religious and patriotic Isabel of Castile. Under the reign of the Catholic Monarchs, as Pope Alexander VI entitled them, a single Spain was created, comprising most of the nation we know today, though the component parts of the newly united kingdom retained their individuality and their institutions.

Aiming to further unite the country, Fernando and Isabel inaugurated the Inquisition in 1478. Initially intended to safeguard religious orthodoxy under Isabel's influential confessor, the fanatical Tomás de Torquemada, it became a byword for the persecution of Jews, Muslims and, later, Protestants. Several thousand suspected heretics were horribly tortured and many were publicly burned at *autos da fé* (show trials). In 1492, Torquemada convinced Fernando and Isabel to expel the surviving unconverted Jews – perhaps

---

El Cid

The legend of El Cid, Spain's national folk hero, is recounted in the epic poem *El Cantar de Mío Cid*. Born Rodrigo Díaz de Vivar in around 1040 near Burgos, he was a highly successful soldier of fortune. Vivar at first fought for the kings of Castile in the battle against the Moors. When Sancho II died in mysterious circumstances, Vivar humiliated his successor, Alfonso VI, by forcing him to swear publicly that he had nothing to do with Sancho's death. Exiled for his impudence, Vivar joined the Moors, from whom he received his honorary title, El Cid (Arabic for 'Lord'). El Cid's greatest victory was in 1094, when he led a Christian-Moorish army to take Valencia, where he died in 1099. Encouraged by his death, a Moorish army regrouped to take the city. El Cid's body was propped on his horse and ridden before the defending army, which routed the attackers.

200,000 in all, including some of the country's best-educated and most productive citizens.

The year 1492 was a momentous one for Spanish history. Not only did it witness the expulsion of the Moors and the Jews, but also Europe's discovery of the New World by Genoese explorer Cristobal Colón (Christopher Columbus). Sponsored by Queen Isabel (who, according to legend, pawned her own jewels to raise the money), the expedition and subsequent annexation of the New World territories laid the foundations for Spain's Golden Age.

The Habsburgs

While Fernando and Isabel were Spain personified, their grandson and heir to the throne, Carlos I, born in Flanders in 1500, could barely compose a sentence in Spanish. Through his father, Philip, Duke of Burgundy, he inherited extensive possessions in the Low Countries; he was appointed Holy Roman Emperor (Charles V) in 1519. An unpopular king, Carlos alienated his Spanish subjects by appointing Flemish and Burgundian supporters in key posts such as Archbishop of Toledo and regent during his frequent absences. Carlos's expansionist foreign policies consolidated Burgundy and the Netherlands as Spanish provinces. He also annexed Milan and Naples and drew Spain into a series of costly European wars funded from the seemingly bottomless pit of Spain's New World bounty.

Fernando and Isabel greet Christopher Columbus

In 1556, overwhelmed by his responsibilities, Carlos

Madrid's elegant Retiro Park, transformed from a former Habsburg hunting ground by Spain's Bourbon rulers

abdicated in favour of his son, Felipe II. Born and educated in Spain, the new king gave top jobs to Castilians and proclaimed Madrid his capital, thereby converting an unimpressive town of 15,000 into the powerhouse of the greatest empire of the age. As literature and the arts flourished, Felipe worked endlessly to administer his over-extended territories. He captured Portugal, and shared in the glory following the destruction of the Turkish fleet at Lepanto (1571). However, the destruction of the Spanish fleet in the disastrous Armada episode (1588) and the spiralling cost of maintaining the empire eventually robbed Felipe of his health and severely depleted the Spanish treasury. He died in devout seclusion at El Escorial, the palace-monastery in the hills northwest of Madrid.

Although Spain was still the dominant force in Europe at Felipe's death, the Golden Age and empire were on the wane. Felipe III delegated his responsibilities to his favourites, involved Spain in the Thirty Years' War between the Catholic and the Protestant parts of Europe, and expelled the remaining *Moriscos* (Moorish converts to Christianity after the Reconquest), many of them farmers, thereby precipitating an agricultural crisis.

The final century of the Habsburg era saw a gradual, then a rapid decline in Spanish fortunes. Ironically, in contrast to the severe loss of territorial possessions and despite the ravages of war, pestilence and famine, the works of Velázquez, Zurbarán, Murillo and Ribera bear witness to the achievements of Spanish artists of the age.

The last of the Spanish Habsburgs, Carlos II, died heirless in 1700. His crown went to the Duke of Anjou, grandson of Louis XIV of France, who claimed the title as Felipe V of Spain. Archduke Charles of Austria (another Habsburg) contested the claim, which sparked the War of the Spanish Succession, ended by the Treaty of Utrecht in 1713.

Bourbons on the Throne

Felipe V eventually secured the throne, but his diminishing empire was now shorn of Belgium, Luxembourg, Milan, Sicily and Sardinia. To add insult to injury, Britain snatched strategic Gibraltar. The most successful Spanish king of the 18th century, Carlos III, recruited capable administrators, disbanded the Inquisition, invigorated the economy and paved the streets of Madrid. But Spain came increasingly under the power of France during the Bourbon period.

After the defeat of the Franco-Spanish fleet by the British at the Battle of Trafalgar in 1805, Carlos IV had to abdicate. Napoleon tried to appoint his brother Joseph as José I, but the Spanish rose against the French, resulting in the Peninsular War (known in Spain as the War of Independence). In

1814, with the help of British troops led by the Duke of Wellington, the French were finally ousted. While all this was going on, a number of Spain's most profitable American colonies took advantage of her preoccupation to secure their independence.

With Fernando VII on the throne, a Bourbon king once again ruled Spain, but the country miserably failed to prosper. Political infighting, a repressive monarchy and anti-clerical revolts led to the domestic Carlist Wars. The 19th century ended with another disaster as Cuba, Puerto Rico and the Philippines were lost in the Spanish-American War.

The Spanish Civil War

Italian planes bomb the Republicans in the Civil War

Spain escaped the horrors of World War I, watching the carnage from a position of neutrality. Alfonso XIII backed the dictatorship of General Miguel Primo de Rivera (1923–30), but went into exile (never to return) after anti-royalist forces won a landslide victory in the 1931 elections. The new Republic was riven with bitter ideological conflicts, particularly between the Left and Right. A left-wing victory in the 1936 elections and the assassination of the Monarchist leader, Calvo Sotelo, ignited nationalist and conservative fears of a Marxist revolution.

WHERE TO GO

MADRID

Settled by the Romans in the 2nd century BC, **Madrid** was occupied by the Moors in AD711. Under Mohammed I, the Moors fortified the town in 865, and made it a walled city. Just over two centuries later, in 1083, Madrid was re-conquered by King Alfonso VI. Fernando IV summoned the Courts of the Kingdom in 1309, the Catholic Monarchs ordered the de-fortification of the city's walls and gates in 1476 and, in 1561, Felipe II moved the court to here from Toledo, thus making Madrid the capital of a vast empire.

The early part of the next century, during the Habsburg era, saw the important addition of the Plaza Mayor. The House of Bourbon succeeded the Habsburgs, and it was this dynasty that was responsible for many of the grand buildings and monuments that adorn the city today. Among these are the Royal Palace, completed in 1764; the Alcalá gate, raised in 1778 to honour Carlos III's entry into the city as king, and the Prado Museum constructed between 1785 and 1819. During the Spanish Civil War, from November 1936 to March 1939, the city was subject to a siege by the Nationalist forces, whose eventual entry into Madrid effectively ended hostilities.

Madrid is the largest city in Spain and, at an elevation of 655m (2,100ft), the highest capital in Europe. The ambiance of this hustling, bustling modern city reflects an intriguing blend of old and new. It also makes a good base for exploring several historic nearby cities. The best way to get around town is by the cheap and efficient *metro* (underground) system.

There is much to see, and the best place to start is the bustling **Puerta del Sol** (Gate of the Sun), the hub of 10 con-

The Casa de la Panadería on Madrid's Plaza Mayor

Sitting out on the vast Plaza Mayor

verging streets. This is literally the crossroads of Spain, known as 'Kilometre 0' in the country's highway system, and home to an imposing equestrian statue of Carlos III and a smaller statue depicting Madrid's coat-of-arms – a bear standing against a *madroño* (arbutus, or strawberry) tree.

Plaza Mayor

A few blocks west is the **Plaza Mayor** (Main Square), a 17th-century architectural masterpiece. Its broad arcades surround a vast, traffic-free, cobbled rectangle, once used as the inner-city showground for bullfights, pageants and even public executions. Today, an equestrian statue of Felipe II surveys rows of outdoor cafés and lively summer-season festivals. The plaza's most famous houses are the **Casa de la Panadería** (Bakers' Guild), which holds some of the city archives, and the **Casa de la Carnicería** (Butchers' Guild), whose façades are decorated with a series of vibrant, and even mildly erotic, paintings.

Continuing west on Calle Mayor, **Plaza de la Villa** juxtaposes stately 16th- and 17th-century buildings of differing styles. These include the lovely **Casa de Cisneros**, which belongs to the ornate and delicate style of architecture known as Plateresque (*platero* means silversmith), and the towering Habsburg-era **Ayuntamiento** (City Hall).

Palacio Real

To the north is the **Palacio Real** (Royal Palace; open Apr–Sept: Mon–Sat 9am–6pm, Sun and holidays 9am–3pm; Oct–Mar Mon–Sat 9.30am–5pm, Sun and holidays 9am–2pm; admission fee; closed on state occasions), set among formal gardens on a bluff overlooking the Manzanares Valley. Felipe V commissioned this imposing French-style palace on the site of the old Moorish fort, and furnished its 2,000 rooms (more than any other European palace except the Hermitage in St Petersburg) in a suitably regal fashion. It was the principal residence of Spanish kings from Felipe's time in the mid-18th century until Alfonso XIII was exiled in 1931. Visit at your leisure, or join one of the hour-long tours that take in around 50 rooms, including the overwhelmingly rococo Gasparini Room, the Ceremonial Dining Room with seating for 145 guests, and the Throne Room with its stunning Tiepolo ceiling frescoes. Also worth seeing are the Royal Armoury, the Pharmacy and the Library.

Guards at the Palacio Real

The **Gran Vía** is Madrid's main thoroughfare. Lined with shops, hotels, restaurants, theatres, cafés and

Diego de Acedo (1644), by Velázquez, in the Museo del Prado

nightclubs, it cuts a wide path west to east from Plaza de España to the busy round **Plaza de la Cibeles**, so named for the Cybele Fountain that is adorned with a sculpture of a Greek fertility goddess.

Art Collections

Art lovers are spoilt for choice in Madrid. One of the city's fascinating hidden treasures is the **Monasterio de las Descalzas Reales** (open: Tues–Thur and Sat 10.30am–12.45pm and 4–5.45pm; Fri 10.30am–12.45pm; Sun and holidays 11am–1.45pm; guided tours), located behind the El Corte Ingles store at the Puerto del Sol. Once a retreat for the Kings of Castile, this 16th-century convent has been handsomely endowed with a wealth of art treasures. The **Real Academía de Bellas Artes de San Fernando**, also close to the Puerto del Sol, has a fine collection of paintings by Goya (open: Tues–Fri 9am–7pm; Sat–Mon and holidays 9am–2.30pm; admission fee, free on Wed except holidays).

Housed in 18th-century neoclassical grandeur, the **Museo del Prado** (open: Tues–Sun 9am–8pm; admisson fee, free Sun), with its fabulous art treasures amassed by the Spanish monarchy, is not to be missed. The Prado houses the world's greatest collection of Spanish paintings, and a particularly strong set of Italian and Flemish masterpieces. If time is short, plan ahead and decide what you most want to see. Likely top-of-the-list sights are works by El Greco (1541–1614), Ribera (1591–1652), Zurbarán (1598–1664), Felipe IV's court painter Velázquez (1599–1660, whose *Las Meninas*, or *Maids of Honour*, is said to be Spain's favourite painting), Murillo (1617–82), and magnificent Goya (1746–1828). Of the Dutch and Flemish masters, be sure not to miss works by Hieronymous Bosch (known as 'El Bosco') and Rubens. The Italian Old Masters include works by Raphael, Titian and Tintoretto.

Directly opposite the main museum, the **Museo Thyssen-Bornemisza** (open: Tues–Sun 10am–7pm; admission fee) spans 700 years of artistic endeavour from the Italian primitives to Pop Art. Just a short distance to the south the **Centro de Arte Reina Sofía** (open: Mon–Sat 10am–9pm, Sun 10am–2.30pm; admission fee, free on Sat after 2.30pm and on Sun am) has important collections of modern art and many masterpieces by Picasso – including his monumental mural, *Guernica*, inspired by the Civil War bombing of a Basque village.

The impressive **Museo Arqueológico** (open: Tues–Sat 9.30am–8.30pm; Sun 9.30am–2.30pm; admission fee, free Sat after 2.30pm and on Sun) contains the celebrated Celtiberian bust known as *La Dama de Elche* and a wealth of Visigothic treasures discovered at Toledo. In the gardens is a replica of the prehistoric Altamira caves *(see page 86)*, complete with wall paintings.

Art lovers intent on seeing Madrid's Big Three art museums – the Prado, Thyssen-Bornemisza, and the Reina Sofía – would do well to acquire the Paseo del Arte voucher. This allows visits to all three museums for a single price (around €8), a considerable saving on the individual admission prices.

If the sightseeing and the bustle get too much, the enormous **Parque del Retiro** behind the Prado is a favourite spot for *Madrileño*s out for a stroll. Originally a 17th-century Habsburg hunting ground, it offers 121 hectares (300 acres) of leafy avenues, flower beds and park benches, including a rose garden, boating lake and Sunday morning sideshows. There are also cafés, exhibitions in the Palacio de Cristal and Palacio de Velázquez and, across the road, a botanical garden founded by Carlos III in 1781.

AROUND MADRID

Aranjuez

One of the most popular day-trips from Madrid is to the royal town of **Aranjuez**, 48km (30 miles) south by train or motorway. The best way to get here in summer is from Atocha station on board the Tren de la Fresa, a steam train running along Spain's second-oldest railway line built in 1849. The main reason to make the journey is to stroll in the pleasant formal gardens, laid out for the leisure of the court, which nudge up to the banks of the Río Tajo (River Tagus). It is not hard to see how they could have been the inspiration for Spain's most famous piece of music, Joaquín Rodrigo's *Concierto de Aranjuez*.

Not to be missed is the **Palacio Real**, a royal palace which stands at the heart of Aranjuez. It took shape over 200 years, evolving through the reigns of eight monarchs, but in its present form it is mostly the work of 18th-century baroque inspiration. The guided tour leads visitors through a succession of ornate rooms including the throne room, king's smoking room and porcelain room. From outside the palace two bridges lead over a narrow branch of the river to the **Jardin de la Isla** (Island Garden), which combines Spanish, Flemish and Moorish influences in its classical fountains and clipped hedges.

Toledo is almost surrounded by the River Tagus

Toledo

Located on a strategic hill protected by the encircling River Tagus, **Toledo** is a fascinating historical city and a UNESCO World Heritage Site. Conquered by the Romans in 193BC, Toledo became the political and religious capital of the Visigoths in the 5th century AD after they had overrun the Vandals. After the Moors invaded Spain, in AD711, the city was incorporated into the Córdoba Emirate. When the Emirate disintegrated in 1012, it became the capital of an independent kingdom. In 1085 Alfonso VI of León reconquered Toledo and made it his capital, a status it retained until 1561 when Felipe II, grandson of the Holy Roman Emperor Carlos (Charles) V, moved the capital to Madrid. This marked the beginning of the decline of the importance of Toledo, even though it has remained the seat of the Primate of Spain.

Unquestionably the most important monument in the city is the massive **cathedral** (open: Mon–Sat 10.30am–6.30pm; Sun

2–6.30pm; admission fee). The first one on this site was built jointly by the Visigoth King Recaredo I and the first Bishop of Toledo, San Eugenio. Converted into a mosque by the Moors, it was not until 1227 that King Fernando III, 'the Saint', began construction of the present building. It was not completed until the 16th century and as it incorporates numerous architectural styles it is known as the 'Museum Cathedral'. The **coro** or choir (closed Sun morning) and main altar reredos are marvels of woodcarving. Just behind the main chapel, Narciso Tomé's baroque **Transparente** is an 18th-century masterpiece, and in the **Sala Capitular** (Chapter House) there is an intricate ceiling in the Mudéjar style. If you look up you'll see hats hanging precariously from the vaulting. They are suspended over plaques that indicate tombs of Primates buried below; each hat belonging to the respective Primate.

Don't miss, either, the **Tesoro** (Treasury) with religious artworks, including 18 paintings by El Greco, and Enrique de Arfe's Monstrance. Made of solid silver and gold, it has more than 5,600 parts and weighs a substantial 200kg (430lb).

Dominating the city is the huge **Alcázar** (open: Tues–Sun 9.30am–2pm; admission fee), a fortress destroyed and rebuilt many times since the Roman era. The latest destruction occurred during the Civil War and the fortress houses an **Army Museum** with displays relating to the dramatic 72-day siege.

Toledo Steel

Toledo is famous all over the world for the quality of its steel, and swords have been forged here since Roman times. According to legend, the special property of the steel is inherited from the magical water of the River Tagus (Rio Tajo). Look for damascene steel souvenirs. This is a craft unique to the city, which involves inlaying black steel with decorative gold, copper and silver filigree.

El Greco in Toledo

The painter El Greco is inextricably linked with Toledo. His first commission was to paint the reredos at the Cistercian convent of **Santo Domingo el Antiguo** which, founded in 1085 by King Alfonso VI, is the oldest monastery in Toledo (open: 11am–1.30pm and 4–7pm; closed Sun am; admission fee). More famously, his *Burial of the Count of Orgaz*, a fascinating depiction of local noblemen attending the count's funeral, is on display at the church of **Santo Tomé** (open: daily 10am–7pm; winter until 6pm; admission fee) – also notable for its land-

Armour in Toledo's Army Museum

mark Mudéjar tower. The young boy attending upon the saints is considered to be a likeness of El Greco's son, and on a handkerchief dangling from the boy's pocket he signed his name, Doménico Theotokopouli, and the date, 1583. More of El Greco's work, including a *Crucifixion* with Toledo as the backdrop, can be found at the 16th-century **Museo-Hospital de Santa Cruz** (open: Mon 10am–2pm, 4–6.30pm; Tues–Sat 10am–6.30pm; closed Sun pm; admission fee).

Just downhill from Santo Tomé is a restored 14th-century building El Greco lived in for a number of years. It now forms the **Museo de El Greco** (open: Tues–Sat 10am–2pm and 4–6pm; Sun 10am–2pm; admission fee), and brings together some of El Greco's work, as well as pieces by Murillo.

Nearby is **La Sinagoga del Tránsito** built by Samuel Levi, a 14th-century financier and a friend of King Pedro I of Castile. Muslim artists adorned the walls with intricate filigree and Hebrew inscriptions from the Psalms. The synagogue houses the **Museo Sefardí** (Sephardic Museum; open: Tues–Sat 10am–2pm and 4–6.30pm; Sun 10am–2pm; admission fee). Not far away is the **Santa Maria la Blanca** synagogue, which resembles a mosque and has a simplicity of style that enhances its ambiance.

Just down the street is a fine church with royal connections. Fernando and Isabel, whose emblems of the different realms combined by their marriage lie either side of the altar, built **San Juan de los Reyes** (St John of the Kings) to celebrate victory at the Battle of Toro in 1476. In a mix of Mudéjar, Gothic and Renaissance styles, it was also meant to be the Catholic Monarchs' final resting place. That was before they became enchanted with Granada, the Moors' last stronghold, which was captured in 1492. There is also a superb double-height cloister with elaborate stone carvings.

There are numerous other churches, museums and monuments in Toledo. Don't miss the 10th-century **El Cristo de la Luz** (Christ of the Light), a mosque until the Reconquest and the only building in the city from that era to have survived in its original condition.

The walls of Ávila

Ávila

Situated 112km (70 miles) northwest of Madrid, at an altitude of 1,128m (3,700ft) above sea level, **Ávila** is the highest city in Spain. With origins in the Celtiberian era, it was Christianised in the 1st century AD, and after nearly three centuries of Moorish rule was reconquered by King Alfonso VI in 1085. After the Reconquest the city was repopulated by Christian knights, who began work on what is unquestionably Ávila's most dominant feature: **Las Murallas** – the walls. These are, on average, over 3.6m (12ft) high and 2.7m (9ft) thick. Built into their nearly 2.7-km (1⅔-mile) length are nine gateways and 90 towers. Noblemen were responsible for defending a particular section of the wall. Consequently, many elegantly fortified mansions were built near, or as an integral part of, the walls. Even the 12th- to 16th-century **cathedral**, combining Romanesque, Gothic and Renaissance elements, has a *cimorro* (fortified head) built into the walls.

St Teresa depicted in stained glass, Ávila cathedral

Ávila's spiritual influence is a legacy of St Teresa, who was beatified on 12 March, 1622. She was born here in 1515 and her influence, in the shape of churches, convents and statues, is on display throughout the city. A Catholic visionary and advocate of Carmelite thought, she founded no fewer than 17 convents throughout Spain and wrote prolifically. She lived for 30 years in the **Convento de la Incarnación**, outside the city walls, first as a novice and for the last three years as prioress.

Just outside the city walls, the **Basilica de San Vicente** – commemorating St Vincent of Zaragoza and his two sisters, who were martyred in the 4th century – is noted for an extraordinary tomb topped by a bizarre oriental canopy.

Although some distance away from the town centre, the **Monasterio de Santo Tomás** belonging to the Dominican Order should not be missed. Dating from 1482, it was used frequently by the Catholic Monarchs as a summer residence. Fernando and Isabel's only son, Don Juan, died here at the age of 19 and his impressive sepulchre is in the chapel. Treasures acquired by missionaries on their Far Eastern travels are exhibited here in the Oriental Art Museum.

After viewing Ávila up close, drive or take a bus across the Río Adaja to the monument called **Los Cuatro Postes** (The Four Posts). Curious in itself, it consists of four Doric columns connected by cornices, each of which is decorated with the city's coats-of-arms, with a stone cross in the centre. More importantly, the hill offers a panoramic view of the whole of medieval Ávila, which is especially impressive when floodlit at night.

San Lorenzo de El Escorial

At an elevation of 1,065m (3,494ft) in the foothills of the Sierra de Guadarrama, by the town of El Escorial, 49km (30 miles) northwest of Madrid, you will find a building of absolutely massive proportions. Visible from miles away, the monastery of **San Lorenzo de El Escorial** (open: Tues–Sun 10am–7pm; until 6pm Oct–Mar; admission fee) was commissioned in 1557 by Felipe II to commemorate his victory over Henri II of France at the Battle of San Quentín, an event that took place on 10 August, the Feast Day of San Lorenzo (St Lawrence). Extended over the years, it has 86 stairways, more than 1,200 doors and 2,600 windows, summing up the physical and spiritual superlatives of the empire's Golden Age.

The monastery is actually a multifaceted complex, comprising royal living quarters, a basilica, monastery, pantheon, elaborate library, and art galleries and museum all under one roof. The **apartments of Felipe II** are modest in comfort but rich in art, and include a fantastic triptych by Hieronymus Bosch. The **Palacio Real** (Royal Palace) has a succession of lavishly decorated rooms, notably the Sala de las Batallas, adorned with frescoes depicting complex battle scenes, and fine tapestries. Of the dozens of works of art collected in the great **basilica** – which is part Sotocoro (people's church), part monastic church and part royal – none attracts more admiration than Cellini's life-sized marble crucifix. Felipe II died at the palace in 1598 and, along with the remains of almost all Spain's monarchs and their families from the 17th century onwards, is buried in the elaborately fascinating royal **pantheon**. The

San Lorenzo de El Escorial, where Felipe II lived and died

library, with its baroque ceiling adorned with a series of magnificent frescoes by Tibaldi, is particularly spectacular and contains some 40,000 rare books, plus priceless and beautiful manuscripts. The **New Museums** display masterpieces by Ribera, Tintoretto, Velázquez and El Greco. In 1984 El Escorial was declared a World Heritage Monument by UNESCO.

Valle de los Caidos

Just around the mountain is another monument of enormous proportions, albeit one of a very different type. After the Spanish Civil War, Generalíssimo Franco wanted to build a monument to commemorate those who died during the hostilities. For the site he chose the V-shaped valley called Cuelgamuros, in the Sierra de Guadarrama, known today as the **Valle de los Caidos** (Valley of the Fallen). Of the two disparate parts, the most visible – from miles around – is a huge cross standing 150m (492ft) high and 46m (150ft) wide, set upon the summit of a small mountain. On weekends and holidays a funicular takes visitors to the base of the cross where they may investigate the plinth adorned by four enormous figures.

Valle de los Caidos

Equally grand is the underground **Basilica** (open: Tues–Sun 10am–6.30pm, until 5.30pm Oct–Mar; admission fee). Carved 240m (786ft) deep into the granite mountain, it is reached via a tunnel and opens out into a gigantic dome that is almost directly under the cross outside. The tombstones of Franco and José Antonio

Segovia's skyline and Gothic cathedral from atop the Alcázar

Primo de Rivera, founder of the Falangist Party, occupy a privileged position. A series of Flemish tapestries dating from 1553 decorates the church, and ossuaries in the crypt (closed to the public) contain the remains of tens of thousands of the dead, of both sides, from the Civil War.

Segovia

Segovia, 88km (55 miles) northwest of Madrid, is an unspoiled medieval town that strategically sits on a high promontory between two rivers. High on the rocks overlooking the confluence of the rivers is the **Alcázar** (open: daily summer 10am–7pm; winter 10am–6pm; admission fee), Segovia's fairytale royal castle. Although originally constructed in the 12th and 13th centuries, much of it dates from the following two centuries. It became a royal favourite – Isabel left from here to be proclaimed queen – but was converted to a Royal Artillery School in the late 18th century

Segovia's Roman aqueduct

and was largely rebuilt after a fire in 1862. Today, it houses a museum of weaponry, and you can climb the 152 steps to the top of the tower for spectacular views.

The towering **cathedral** was begun in 1525, after the original one – on a different site – was destroyed during the Comuneros War. As a consequence, it is the last of the great Spanish cathedrals to be built in the Gothic style. Fine stained-glass windows illuminate the interior.

Segovia is best known, though, for the **Roman aqueduct**, both a work of art and a triumph of engineering. Dating from the 1st or 2nd century AD, it has 165 arches covering a length of 728m (2,392ft) and it reaches 28m (92ft) in height. Amazingly, the granite stones are held together by nothing but their own weight.

Segovia has an array of other interesting churches, monasteries and museums, the most interesting of which is a small church, almost within the shadow of the Alcázar. The **Vera Cruz** church dates from the 13th century and was probably founded by the Knights Templar. Its 12-sided design is believed to have been copied from the Church of the Holy Sepulchre in Jerusalem. It is unique in Spain but similar to many other churches that the knights founded in Portugal. Outside Segovia is the royal summer palace of **La Granja de San Ildefonso**, with its magnificent formal gardens.

BARCELONA

Of Phoenician origins, **Barcelona** flourished under the Romans, and remains of the walls constructed during that era are still visible in the city's so-called Gothic Quarter; foundations of the Roman town have been excavated from beneath the City History Museum. The period of Visigothic rule saw a decline in importance and although the Moors swept across the Iberian peninsula in the early 8th century they were unable to control this area for long. In 801, following its recapture by the Franks, the city was incorporated into Charlemagne's empire as the capital of the county of Barcelona, the most dominant of the Catalan counties. For nearly five centuries, unlike in other parts of the country, Barcelona and Catalunya remained Christian, giving this region an entirely different character from the rest of Spain. Subsequently, it was united with the neighbouring kingdom of Aragón in the 12th century, thus ensuing a period of flourishing maritime trade.

The unification of Spain under Fernando of Aragón and Isabel of Castile in 1469 led to attempts to suppress the well-established institutions of this dynamic and strongly independent region. For centuries, Barcelona repeatedly struggled to maintain its unique identity. During the Spanish Civil War it served as the capital of the Republican forces and was almost the last city to fall to Franco. As a result, Barcelona was singled out for

Barcelona's surrealistic Sagrada Família cathedral

harsh reprisals, and the Catalan language was suppressed. Now, with a well-earned reputation for its style and architecture, particularly that of Antoni Gaudí, Barcelona is the thriving capital of a largely autonomous region where the people display a passion for all things Catalan, including their language. The net effect is an ambiance quite different to that in the rest of Spain.

La Rambla

Without doubt, **La Rambla**, linking the popular **Plaça de Catalunya** with the harbour, is Barcelona's most popular street. Everyone comes to walk along its wide tree-lined promenade, with its street artists performing impromptu shows, its living statues posing for photographs, its market stalls and brightly coloured flower kiosks, its open-air

Getting Around Barcelona

Barcelona is the second largest city in Spain, and its many attractions are widely separated from each other. It helps that there is an excellent public transport system, and the buses and metro (underground) will take you almost everywhere you need to go. A neat option is the Bus Turistic, which has two routes – the red northern route and blue southern route (with connections at three stops). Both depart from the Plaça de Catalunya from 9am daily. Each route provides a handy hop-on, hop-off service around all the main sights. Tickets, available on board or at tourist offices, include discounted admission to many museums and attractions, including the cable car, funicular and tram rides for Montjuïc and Tibidabo. Also worth considering is the Barcelona Card, which can be purchased for periods of one to five days and offers free public transport as well as more than 100 discounts at museums, places of entertainment, shops, restaurants and even the Aerobus (airport bus).

restaurants and bars. Along its route are numerous places of interest, including the ever-popular **La Boqueria** – the 19th-century covered market that is a city highlight – and the famous **Liceu** opera house (expanded and completely refurbished after a devasting fire in 1985).

A little further on, Gaudí's fortress-like **Palau Güell**, on Nou de la Rambla, was built for his major sponsor in 1885. And across La Rambla a passage leads into the café-filled arcades of the fine **Plaça Reial**, adorned by a central fountain and iron lanterns, both designed by Gaudí, and no fewer than 35

Dancing on La Rambla

palm trees. Further down, the **Mirador de Colón** – honouring Christopher Columbus (Cristóbal Colón) – towers over the harbour area and is close to the **Museu Marítim** (open: daily 10am–8pm; admission fee), which traces 700 years of Barcelona's maritime history and is well worth a visit just for the architecture of the enormous ship-building sheds.

The harbour area at the end of La Rambla has been completely transformed in recent years. Traditional *golondrinas* boats offer a fun way of seeing the harbour, or you can cross **Port Vell** to the Moll d'Espanya by a wooden promenade. There you'll find a modern complex consisting of shops, restaurants, an IMAX theatre and the **Aquàrium de Barcelona** (open: daily 9.30am–9pm; weekends June–Sept 9.30am–

Plaça Sant Jaume, at the heart of the Barri Gòtic

9pm; July and August 9.30am–11pm; admission fee) – one of Europe's largest and a favourite with children of all ages.

Barri Gòtic

The narrow alleyways and historic buildings of **Barri Gòtic** cluster around the imposing **Catedral** (open: daily 8am–1.15pm and 4.30–7.30pm). The third on the site, it dates from the 13th century but has a 19th-century façade. In the square outside you will see performances of the Catalan national dance on summer weekends; there is also a graceful garden cloister. Nearby are two fascinating museums: the **Museu d'Història de la Ciutat** (open: Tues–Sat 10am–2pm and 4–8pm; June–Sept 10am–8pm; Sun 10am–3pm; admission fee) leads through the underground Roman foundations to the **Palau Reial Major**, the former Royal Palace; the **Museu Frederic Marès** (open: Tues–Sat 10am–7pm, Sun and holidays 10am–3pm; admission fee) contains an eclectic miscellany of religious objects and art from around the world with pieces dating from the Middle Ages.

Among the galleries on Carrer de Montcada, the **Museu Picasso** (open: Tues–Sat 10am–8pm, Sun 10am–3pm; admission fee) is the city's most popular museum. Entrance is through the 15th-century Palau Aguilar, and the collection includes many of Picasso's early works, major pieces from his Blue and Pink periods, the idiosyncratic *Las Meninas* series (based on the Velásquez masterpiece in Madrid's Prado), as well as ceramics. Be sure, also, to pop into the **El Xampanyet** bar at No. 22 where, besides delicious *tapas*, a refreshingly light, sparkling, champagne-like *cava* is served.

The pure, Gothic beauty of the 14th-century **Santa María del Mar** church (open: daily 9.30am–1.30pm and 4.30–8pm; free) can be seen at the bottom of Montcada.

Parc Ciutadella

To the east, the green expanse of the **Parc Ciutadella**, its name derived from an 18th-century prison torn down with much glee in 1869, encompasses paths, gardens and ponds, and an elaborate Gaudí fountain. It also has the Catalan parliament and the **Parc Zoològico**, one of Europe's better zoos, known as the home of Copito de Nieve (Snowflake), the world's only albino gorilla in captivity, who died in 2003, aged forty.

Santa María del Mar

Montjuïc

Barcelona's historic Jewish community once lived on the slopes of Montjuïc (Hill of the Jews), which looms up behind the harbour, crowned by the 17th-century **Castillo de Montjuïc** and reached by cable car, funicular or bus. The castle offers spectacular views of the city and also houses a military museum. Down below is the **Font Mágica** (magic fountain), which is illuminated on summer evenings. Other attractions of the area include the **Fundació Joan Miró** (open: Tues, Wed, Fri, Sat 10am–7pm, until 8pm July–Sept, Thur 10am–9.30pm; Sun and holidays 10am–2.30pm; admission fee), and facilities left from the 1992 Olympic Games including the main stadium, swimming pools and the **Torre de Calatrava** that became one of the symbols of those games. There is also the **Poble Espanyol** (Spanish Village; open: daily from 9am, Mon until 8pm, Tues–Thur to 2am; Fri–Sat to 4am, Sun to midnight; admission fee) which showcases Spanish architecture and traditions with miniature replicas of palaces, castles and churches, plus artisans' workshops, concerts and evening flamenco performances. World-class collections of Romanesque and Gothic art are displayed in the **Museu Nacional d'Art de Catalunya** (open: Tues–Sat 10am–7pm, Sun 10am–2.30pm; admission

Modernisme

Modernisme, a movement related to the design styles in vogue in Europe in the late 19th century – French art nouveau, German and Austrian Jugendstil – was a rebellion against the rigid forms and colourless stone and plaster of classical architecture. In Barcelona the new style assumed nationalist motifs and significance, which may be why it has been so carefully preserved here. Although there was an entire school of *modernista* architects working in Barcelona from the late 19th century until the 1930s, it is customary to speak of the 'Big Three': Antoni Gaudí, who left such a personal mark on the city; Lluís Domènech i Montaner and Josep Puig i Cadafalch.

fee) in the imposing Palacio Nacional, which also contains the **Museu d'Art Modern**, with a notable collection of 19th- and 20th-century Catalan works, as well as *modernista* furniture.

Gaudí's Legacy

Of course, Barcelona is also famous for Antoni Gaudí's unique and eccentric architectural designs. The largest of these is the surrealistic **Sagrada Família** (Holy Family) church (open: daily 9am–6pm, until 8pm in summer; admission fee). An unfinished masterpiece started in 1882 (and still in progress), its 100-m (330-ft) towers are local landmarks.

The rooftops of Gaudí's Casa Milà, also known as La Pedrera

Other Gaudían highlights include tours of the **Casa Milà** rooftops and one of the apartments at Passeig de Gràcia 92 (open: daily 10am–8pm; guided tours available but not obligatory); the **Casa Batlló** (open: Mon–Sat 9am–2pm; Sun 9am–8pm; admission fee) down the street at No. 43; and the fascinating **Park Güell**, with colourful tile mosaics.

Pedralbes

On the western edge of the city, the beautiful **Monastir Santa María de Pedralbes** (open: Tues–Sun 10am–2pm; admission fee) deserves a special mention. Founded by Queen Elisenda in 1326, it has a charming cloister and an

Montserrat monastery

exceptional selection of paintings on loan from the
Thyssen-Bornemisza art collection in Madrid. Last, but by
no means least, the popular amusement park at **Tibidabo**
combines the best in old- and new-technology rides, offering spectacular views from its perfect perch on a 542-m
(1,778-ft) peak in the western hills overlooking Barcelona.

AROUND BARCELONA

Montserrat
Just 40km (25 miles) northwest of Barcelona, and easily
reached by train and cable car, the monastery of **Montserrat**
sits on the ridge of a highly unusual rock formation 1,135m
(3,725ft) above the Llobregat river valley. This is the spiritual home of Catalunya and one of Spain's most important pilgrimage sites thanks to the monastery's Black Madonna – *La
Moreneta* – a statue said to have been made by St Luke and

brought to Barcelona by St Peter. In 1808, Napoleon's troops destroyed the original 12th-century monastery and the present building dates from 1874.

Montserrat is still an active Benedictine monastery; visitors may only enter the beautiful Gothic cloister, the basilica, and the museum. A highlight of any visit is a recital by the famous Escalonia Boys' Choir (Mon–Sat at 1pm and 7.10pm), while the **museum** features art by El Greco, Picasso and modern Catalan artists, as well as interesting archaeological treasures. Tourists to this popular site are fully catered for, and local stalls sell honey and cheese. It is easy to escape the crowds by following one of the four well-signposted hermitage walks through Montserrat's magnificent protected mountain parkland. One of these goes to the **Santa Cova** (the Holy Cave) where *La Moreneta* was allegedly discovered.

Poblet

Travel 133km (83 miles) west of Barcelona to find the largest and best-preserved Cistercian monastery in Europe (open: daily 10am–12.30pm and 3–6pm; admission fee). The monastery was founded in 1151 by Ramon Berenguer, the Count of Barcelona, as a gesture of thanksgiving for the reconquest of Catalunya. Poblet's façade is a majestic sight, and once inside a guided tour leads past the wine cellars, library, chapter house and refectory into the Romanesque and Gothic-style church and its spacious rose-garden cloister.

Poblet's Gothic chapel, burial place of Catalan monarchs

Tarragona

This town, 95km (60 miles) south of Barcelona, was the site of an ancient Iberian settlement, but it was the Romans, in the 3rd century BC, who established it as an important military and political base. Tarraco, as it was then known, quickly grew to a population of 30,000 and minted its own currency. By 27BC it was the capital of Tarraconensis, the largest Roman province on the Iberian peninsula. The town now has some of the finest Roman remains to have survived in Spain.

The Rambla Vella (Old Rambla) neatly divides Tarragona in half. To the north is the old walled city, while to the south is the Rambla Nova (New Rambla) and the modern part of town. At the end of the Rambla Vella the **Balco del Mediterrani** looks down onto Tarragona's commercial port, one of the busiest in the Mediterranean. The adjacent port is worthy of a visit for its fish restaurants.

Tarragona's Roman amphitheatre

To get a glimpse of the old city, you can take a walk along the **Passeig Arqueològic**. This follows the top of the old city walls, which enclose a maze of charming medieval streets. The upper levels of the ramparts were built by the Romans above huge cyclopean boulders, supposedly placed there by Iberian tribes in the 6th century BC. In this part of town, the **Museu Arqueològic** in Plaça del Rei has a modern, well-designed exhibition of delicate mosaics and other ancient artefacts. Next door, the **Pretori Romà** (Roman Praetorium) is thought to have been part of the original complex belonging to the provincial administration. It was restored in the Middle Ages and today houses the atmospheric **Museu d'Història** (History Museum). Walking from here towards the sea brings you to the ruins of both the Roman **amphitheatre**, built into the hillside, and the 12th-century **Santa María del Miracle** church. Gladiators fought here and Spain's first Christian martyr died here in AD259.

Medieval Tarragona's pride and joy is its **cathedral**, the largest in Catalunya, founded in 1171 but not consecrated until 1333. The 12th- to 13th-century cloister is an attraction in its own right, while the **Museu Diocesà** has a fine collection of art treasures and Flemish tapestries.

Tarragona's most important ancient site beyond the old city walls, the **Necròpolis i Museu Paleocristiàns** (Necropolis and Paleo-Christian Museum), stands at the site of the city's early Christian burial ground. Excavations have uncovered more than 2,000 graves; you will find the best archaeological discoveries displayed in the museum.

Tarragona's most impressive Roman monument, the first-century **Pont del Diable**, is some 4km (2½ miles) north of the town centre, off the N240 towards Lleida (Lérida). The 'Devil's Bridge' is actually a perfectly preserved two-storey aqueduct, which spans 217m (712ft) and rises to a height of 27m (88ft) above the ground.

Andalusian landscape surrounding the historic town of Antequera in the mountains north of Málaga

ANDALUCÍA

Andalucía is the southernmost autonomous region of Spain, stretching from the Atlantic and Portuguese border in the west to the Mediterranean south of Murcia in the east. It consists of eight provinces: Huelva, Cádiz, Málaga, Granada and Almería west to east along the coastline, and Sevilla, Córdoba and Jaén landlocked to the north. It has a magnificent array of scenery, including the Sierra Nevada – the highest peaks in mainland Spain – the alluvial plains of the Guadalquivir river, the deserts of Almería and the *pueblos blancos* (white villages) of the interior. Epitomised by its bullfighting and flamenco dancing, Andalucía is considered by many to be the soul of Spain. Its face has been moulded by both Spanish and Arabic cultures, and the fascinating mix of the two can be found all over the region, as well as in the great cities of Córdoba, Granada and Sevilla.

Sevilla

When Julius Caesar arrived in Spain in 45BC, **Sevilla** was a thriving riverside settlement, but under the Romans it became a major town. Two Roman emperors – Hadrian and Trajan – were born in nearby Itálica. Subsequently capital of the Visigoths and then of a Moorish *taifa*, Sevilla finally fell to King Fernando III in 1248. A monopoly of trade with the New World brought the city to its peak during the Golden Age. 'Madrid is the capital of Spain,' the saying went, 'but Sevilla is the capital of the world.' Without doubt, Sevilla, the capital of Andalucía and Spain's fourth largest city, is the most important city in the region. Its name is evocative of bullfighting, flamenco, the operatic temptress Carmen and many icons that represent Spain in visitors' minds. It is also a truly beautiful city.

The city's two most prominent monuments are located around the Plaza del Triunfo. The **cathedral** (open: Mon-Sat 11am–5pm, Sun 2.30–6pm; admission fee includes entry to the Giralda, free on Sun) is the largest Gothic church in the world, and among cathedrals is only surpassed in size by St Peter's in Rome and St Paul's in London. It was begun in 1401 after the great mosque was razed and completed in just over a century. The new building followed the ground plan of the old mosque, accounting for its unusual broad, rectangular form. Massive without, and richly decorated within, the cathedral contains more than 30 chapels, including the central **Capilla Mayor**

Sevilla's cathedral with the Giralda tower

with its Flemish Plateresque altarpiece, and the **Capilla Real** (Royal Chapel), last resting place of Fernando III, the 'King-Saint' who delivered Sevilla from the hands of the infidel. The stunning altar screen is overlaid with 3,500kg (7,716lb) of gold. Christopher Columbus (Cristobal Colón) is interred in the ornate 19th-century sarcophagus by the south entrance. His remains were transferred to Sevilla from Havana in 1898, when Cuba won its independence from Spain.

On the north side of the cathedral is the **Patio de los Naranjos** (Court of the Orange Trees), the ceremonial courtyard of the old mosque with its original ablutions fountains. The bell tower of the cathedral, the celebrated **Giralda** tower – Sevilla's most famous landmark – dates from 1184, and was the original mosque's minaret. The exterior is beautifully decorated with typical *sebka* design work, while the interior has a series of 35 gently rising ramps (designed for horses to climb – Fernando III rode his horse to the top following the Reconquest in 1248) leading to an observation platform 70m (230ft) in the air and offering a tremendous panorama across the city.

Sevilla's Jardines de los Alcázares

The **Alcázar** is a major monument of mid-14th century Mudéjar architecture, combining Moorish, Gothic and Renaissance elements (open Apr–Sept: Tues–Sat 9.30am–8pm, Sun 9.30am–6pm; Oct–Mar: Tues–Sat 9.30am–6pm, Sun 9.30am–2.30pm; admission fee). Built by Moorish craftsmen under Christian rule, during the reign of Pedro the Cruel, the rambling palace and its several courtyards incorporate fragments of an earlier Moorish fortress, and blend Christian motifs with Moorish designs. Not to be missed are the extensive and beautiful gardens, an oasis of tranquillity in this perpetually busy city.

> **The colourful glazed ceramic tiles *(azulejos)* that you see in Sevilla owe their origins to the Moors, who adorned their palaces with mosaics in sophisticated geometric patterns. (The word *azulejo* derives from the Arabic for 'little stone'.)**

Nearby, on the banks of the river, is another of Sevilla's icons. The Moorish **Torre del Oro** (Tower of Gold) is named after the gold-coloured tiles that once covered the walls of this early 13th-century tower – all that remains of Sevilla's medieval fortifications.

Bordering on the Alcázar, the labyrinthine streets of the **Barrio de Santa Cruz** exude history and charm. On the border of this district, more Mudéjar sensations await in the 16th-century **Casa de Pilatos** (open: daily 9am–6pm, until 7pm Mar–Sept; admission fee, free Tues 1–5pm).

Other places not to miss are the **Hospital de la Caridad** (Charity Hospital), the **Plaza de España**, the **Bullfighting Museum and Plaza de Toros**, the **Museo de Bellas Artes** (open: Tues 2.30–8.30pm, Wed–Sat 9am–8.30pm, Sun 9am–2.30pm; admission fee) with its impressive art collection, and the site of Roman **Itálica**, 10km (6 miles) to the northwest.

Córdoba

Córdoba was the largest city in Roman Spain, the capital of the province of Baetica, and birthplace of Seneca the Younger, philosopher and tragedian. But its golden era was between the mid-8th and very early 11th centuries, when it was the centre of the great medieval Caliphate of Córdoba. As one of the world's largest and most cultured cities, the

Inside La Mezquita, Córdoba

splendid capital of the western Islamic Empire had the first university and the earliest street lighting in Europe.

The city is dominated by the greatest surviving monument from that period, the magnificent Great Mosque known as **La Mezquita** (open Mon–Sat 10am–7.30pm, Sun 9am–10.15pm 2–7.30pm; admission fee). Its beauty and power are breathtaking. Begun in 786, it was enlarged three times before attaining its present size, covering an area of 2 hectares (5 acres), in 987. Córdoba was reconquered in 1236, and two small Christian chapels were added in 1258 and 1260. In the early 16th century Carlos V constructed a Christian cathedral in the centre of the mosque. With heavy ornamentation, a blaze of colour and human images in paint, stone and wood, it contrasts shockingly with the understated simplicity – and lack of human images – of Islamic design. Set in the southeast wall is the splendid 10th-century **mihrab** (the niche pointing towards Mecca) lined with marble and gold mosaics, and the **maksourah**, the enclosure where the caliph attended to his prayers.

A Christian king, Alfonso XI, built Córdoba's **Alcázar de los Reyes Cristianos** (open: Tues–Sat 8.30am–2.30pm; Sun 9.30–2.30pm; admission fee), and there are patios, Roman relics, terraced gardens, and ramparts with fine views.

Fernando and Isabel received Columbus and planned the invasion of Granada while they were in residence here.

Also well worth a visit are the 14th-century **synagogue** in the **Barrio de la Judería** (Jewish Quarter), the 16th-century **Palacio de los Marquéses de Viana**, with 13 flower-filled patios that are so typical of Córdoba, the **Plaza de la Corredera** dating from the 17th century and the only Castilian-style plaza in Andalucía, the **Museo Arqueológico** and the **Museo Taurino**. Look, also, for the unusual Plaza del Potro, home to the **Museo Diocesano de Bellas Artes** (Fine Arts Museum) and the **Museo Julio Romero de Torres**.

Granada

The Nasrid dynasty rose to power in Granada just as the fortunes of the Spanish Moors were beginning to wane, when Mohammed ben Alhamar established his capital here in 1232, after Fernando III had forced him from Jaén. Two years later, Moors fleeing from the newly vanquished Sevilla swelled the population, which had already been augmented by refugees from Córdoba. These industrious Moors set about making Granada the grandest city of Andalucía, creating the sumptuous hilltop palace of the Alhambra. Granada was the last of the great Moorish kingdoms of Andalucía to be reconquered, having survived more than 250 years longer than the others, and King Boabdil's surrender to the Catholic Monarchs in January 1492 marked the end of the Muslim Empire in Spain.

**Patio de Arrayanes
in the Alhambra**

➤ The second most visited monument in Spain, the world-famous **Alhambra** (meaning 'The Red') takes its name from the red-brown bricks used in the construction of its outer walls (open: 8.30am–8pm; admission fee). Rising precipitously above the deep gorge of the River Darro, these have the towering – and often snow-covered – peaks of the Sierra Nevada as a backdrop.

There are four main areas to explore at the Alhambra: the Alcazaba, Palacios Nazaríes, Palacio de Carlos V and the Generalife. The Alcazaba (fortress) is the oldest section, with towers dating back to the mid-13th century. From the top of the **Torre de la Vela** (Watchtower) there are excellent views over the modern city below. The Nazrid Palaces (also open in the evenings: Tues–Sat 10–11.30pm) lie at the heart of the Alhambra. The intricacy and bountiful beauty of the designs here create a visual impression that is beyond mere words.

The highlights are the **Salón de Embajadores** (Hall of the Ambassadors), or royal audience chamber, one of the most sumptuously ornamented rooms in the Alhambra; the **Patio de los Leones**, the name of which derives from the splashing fountain in the centre upheld by 12 stone lions; the **Torre de las Damas** (Tower of the Ladies); and the old bathing area.

Visiting the Alhambra

To protect the Alhambra, admission numbers are controlled. Tickets are limited and sold according to availability. You can avoid queuing or disappointment if you book in advance (minimum a day, maximum a year ahead) using the BBVA reservation system: tel: 902 224 460; outside Spain (34) 91 537 9178. You pay by credit card, are given a code number and collect from a BBVA branch or the Alhambra ticket office. Alternatively, book through <www.alhambratickets.com>. For all latest information visit <www.alhambra-patronato.es>.

The Alhambra glows red beneath the Sierra Nevada

The **Palacio de Carlos V** was commissioned in 1527 by Carlos V; square on the outside, it has a surprisingly elegant two-storey circular patio inside. The palace houses the **Museo de la Alhambra** (open: Tues–Sat 9am–2pm) and the **Museo de Bellas Artes** (Fine Arts Museum).

The **Generalife**, at the eastern end of the Alhambra fortifications, is a modest summer palace surrounded by beautiful terraced gardens, where oleander and roses bloom luxuriantly, and delicate fountains and cascades play among the neatly clipped cypress hedges. The complex was allowed to fall into disrepair over the centuries, and it was not until 1870 that it was designated a National Monument.

Facing the Alhambra hill, the **Albaicín**, Granada's oldest and most picturesque quarter, is fun to explore, affording glimpses of the Alhambra between whitewashed houses, outdoor restaurants and cafés. At the bottom of the hill are some Arab baths.

Back down in the city the most prominent monument is the exquisite **Capilla Real** (Royal Chapel), a Renaissance chapel that serves as the mausoleum of the Catholic Monarchs, as well as their daughter, Juana La Loca, and her husband, Felipe El Hermoso. Their mortal remains were interred in the crypt below in 1521, after a ceremonial transfer from the Alhambra. On show in the **sacristy** are mementos of the Catholic Monarchs, including Fernando's sword and Isabel's sceptre and crown, a circle of gold embellished with acanthus scrolls.

Jerez de la Frontera

The largest town in the province of Cádiz, the fame of Jerez is based upon sherry and horses. The English corrupted Jerez to 'sherry' and exported the locally produced wine. Several of the many *bodegas* (wineries) in Jerez welcome tourists to their dark, aromatic halls, and offer free tastings. As for the horses, the **Real Escuela Andaluza del Arte Ecuestre** (Royal Andalucían School of Equestrian Art) puts its star pupils through a beautifully choreographed dressage show at noon every Tuesday and Thursday, and there are weekday training sessions and sometimes special galas. The highlight of the equestrian calendar is the May Spring Horse Fair, when the town is full of dandified horses and their elaborately dressed riders.

At a bodega in Jerez

An 11th-century mosque is found inside the **Alcázar fortress**, and the nearby 18th-century Colegiata holds a precious image of Christ of the Vineyards. Among the other attractions, look especially for the **Museo de Arte Flamenco** in the distinguished Palacio de Penmartin and the **Clock Museum** in La Atalaya Palace

> In Andalucía the palest and driest styles of sherry – *manzanilla* and *fino* – are drunk well chilled as an appetiser or an accompaniment to *tapas*.

Carmona

Carmona has a history that dates back to the neolithic period 5,000 years ago. It was the Roman era, though, that brought the area prosperity and wealth, and the **Museo y Necropolis** is the largest Roman necropolis outside Rome. Carmona was never under feudal rule, and was protected as a 'Crown' city; consequently it has an extraordinary number of palaces, mansions, convents and churches. It also has two formidable gates that linked the old *card maxim* (the Roman road).

Ronda

Dramatically clinging to a cliff-top 150m (500ft) above the Tajo Gorge, **Ronda** was an Iberian then a Roman settlement. Under the Moors it proved impregnable for seven centuries. The **Puente Nuevo** spans the gorge and connects the new centre with the old town, from where Ronda's Moorish kings and its Christian conquerors ruled at the **Palacio de Mondragón**. Behind a Renaissance portal, the elegant courtyards, horseshoe arches and Arabic inscriptions reveal the origins of this stately structure that now houses the town museum. The town's former main mosque survives a short walk away as the **Santa María la Mayor** church.

Back across the bridge, seek out the perfect neoclassical **Plaza de Toros** (bullring), one of the oldest in Spain and venerated as the cradle of the *corrida (see page 136)*. It was a Ronda man, Francisco Romero, who spelled out the rules

Ronda's Plaza de Toros is one of the oldest in Spain

of bullfighting in the 18th century. There's a small museum here that is of interest to the non-aficionado.

Medina Azahara

Eight kilometres (5 miles) west of Córdoba are the ruins of the intriguing Medina Azahara city/palace, commissioned in 936 by Abdel-Rahman III in honour of his favourite concubine Al Zahra (The Flower). It had a short life because it was razed with the breakup of the Caliphate of Córdoba in the early 11th century. For nearly 900 years it was left in ruins, and not until 1910 did the slow work of excavating begin, exposing a city covering an area 1,500 x 750m (4,920 x 2,460ft), and enclosed by a wall fortified by towers. Excavation still continues, but reconstructed **royal apartments** give some impression of the original magnificence of this sumptuous complex of baths, schools, gardens and stately apartments built on three terraces.

The White Towns

Andalucía is at its most picturesque in the brilliant white-washed villages and towns *(pueblos blancos)* that dot the mountains between Málaga and Cádiz. Many of them are spectacularly located high on hillsides or under the walls of crumbling castles. All are higgledy-piggledy labyrinths of tapering streets, steps and shady alleyways which have changed little since they were inhabited by Spain's Moorish population in the middle ages. The best known of them is Ronda *(see page 63)*. Two other good bases for exploring the area are **Arcos de la Frontera** and **Grazalema**. Perhaps the prettiest of the white towns is **Zahara de la Sierra**.

Baeza and Úbeda

These beautifully preserved twin towns, separated by a small valley, flourished as Christian strongholds during the Reconquest. **Baeza**, with more than 50 listed historical buildings, is the smaller of the two. **Úbeda** is just as engaging, and its showcase square, the **Plaza Vázquez de Molina**, is surrounded by a host of magnificent Renaissance palaces and churches. The town hall is housed in the **Palacio de las Cadenas** (Palace of Chains), so called for the chains round its forecourt, and the stunningly rich domed **Sacra Capilla del Salvador** (Chapel of the Holy Saviour) is the town's finest church. The **Hospital de Santiago**, designed by Andrés de Vandelvira, with its graceful Renaissance courtyard, is also well worth seeing.

Sculpture at Úbeda's Hospital de Santiago

Tossa de Mar on the Costa Brava

THE COSTAS

From the Costa Brava at the eastern end of the Pyrenees all the way round to the Costa de la Luz and the border with Portugal, the famous Spanish *costas* attract millions of holidaymakers every year. The coastline stretches for some 2,500km (1,562 miles) from the sheltered Mediterranean to the blustery Atlantic. There are rocky coves and glorious stretches of golden sand, family resorts and jet-set ports. In spite of the much-reported ravages of extensive development and building, you can still find many charming spots along the coast. The *costas* – not now always as cheap and cheerful as they once were – offer a sun-and-fun atmosphere that will always be a major attraction.

The Costa Brava
Stretching from the French border to just north of Barcelona, this is perhaps the prettiest coastline in Spain. Package

tourism arrived here in the early 1960s, but the cliffs and coves of the 'Wild Coast' still conceal a handful of traditional fishing villages and secluded beaches in the north of the region. You will find the major tourism development concentrated in the south (at Lloret de Mar, for instance).

Cadaqués may look like a typical whitewashed fishermen's village, but it attracts a distinctly atypical crowd of chic, monied holidaymakers. Although it is still a working port, without a decent beach, the village has developed into something of an artists' haunt. In fact, Salvador Dalí built a modest retreat here on the edge of Cadaqués at Port Lligat in 1929. The bizarre house that he and his wife Gala created out of a series of fishermen's cottages is now open to the public as the **Casa-Museu Salvador Dalí** (open: mid-June–mid-Sept daily 10.30am–9pm; mid-Mar–mid-June and mid-Sept–early Jan Tues–Sun 10.30am–6pm; admission fee). Visitor numbers are strictly controlled and prior booking is essential, tel: (34) 972 251 015, e-mail: <pllgrups@dali-estate.org>.

Dalí in Figueres

Born in Figueres (Figueras), 30km (19 miles) west of Cadaqués, in 1904, the Surrealist artist Salvador Dalí endowed his home town with the suitably surreal **Teatre-Museu Dalí** (open: July–Sept daily 9am–7.45pm; Oct–June Tues–Sun 10.30am–5.45pm). The second most visited museum in Spain (after the Prado), it is a typically outrageous Dalíesque project. A municipal theatre was gutted, its stage filled with bizarre sculptures, and an ancient Cadillac supporting a statue of a gilt-breasted Amazon was parked on the patio. There are giant models of hens' eggs on the battlements, a roofline topped by a geodesic dome, and Dalí's version of the Sistine Chapel – a homage to Mae West, with her lips replaced by a voluptuous red sofa. Shocks and humour aside, the museum represents an intriguing cross-section of Dalí's work.

Empúries was built by the Greeks, improved by the Iberians, and then greatly expanded by the Romans. The site was perpetually occupied for some 1,500 years. An archaeologist's delight, excavations have uncovered the remains of the villas, temples and marketplaces of these different civilisations. You will also find lovely sea views. The most sensational find was a statue of Asclepius, the Greek god of medicine, which was sculpted in marble from an Athenian quarry. The original has been removed to Barcelona, but a copy stands in the ruined temple. The on-site **museum** displays local finds, from ceramics and jewels to household items and weapons.

The **Medes Islands** off the brash resort of L'Estartit are a nature reserve popular with snorkellers and scuba divers. You can also sail around on a glass-bottom boat.

The most scenic and unspoilt stretch of the Costa Brava is from Begur to Tossa de Mar, a series of cliffs punctuated by coves concealing pretty beaches, such as those of **Aigua Blava**, **Sa Tuna**, **Tamariu Llafranc** and **Calella de Palafrugell**. **Tossa de Mar** itself was an artists' colony before it metamorphosed into a fully developed international resort. The town remains surprisingly attractive, its **Vila Vella** (Old Town) enclosed by brooding 12th-century walls and guarded by three great towers. The **museum** here contains paintings by Marc Chagall and works by other artists who visited the town.

Girona is the inland gateway to the Costa Brava, and is a pleasant day-trip destination from the coast 30km (20 miles) west. The old town is fun to explore, with its typical medieval streets such as **Carrer de la Força**, once the heart of the Jewish quarter. Gerona's Gothic **cathedral** is said to have the widest nave in the world at 22m (72ft), and the treasury, the **Museu Capitular**, is crammed with precious gold and silverwork, rare illuminated manuscripts, statuary and an extraordinary 11th-century tapestry of the Creation. The 12th-century **Banys Arabs** (Arab Baths) nearby are not Arabic at all, but they are intriguing nevertheless.

The Costa Dorada

Stretching from just north of Barcelona to the Ebro Delta, the Costa Dorada derives its name from the fine golden (*daurada*) sand beaches that stretch almost without a break for 241km (150 miles) south of Barcelona. (The city of Tarragona, midway down the coast, is covered in Around Barcelona – *see page 52*).

Sitges, a sophisticated and attractive resort, popular with young weekenders from Barcelona, retains much of its old-world charm and the old town is built around a promontory. Here stands the **Museu Maricel**, which houses a fine collection of paintings and *objets d'art* from around the world, and

The bustling resort of Sitges

offers romantic sea views through picture windows. Adjacent **Cau Ferrat** (Iron Lair) houses one of Spain's most exquisite small museums. Works by El Greco and Picasso, ceramics, crystal and much more are imaginatively displayed. Another good museum, full of knick-knacks, is the **Museu Romàntic**, in an aristocratic mansion lavishly decorated in 19th-century style. (All three open Tues–Sun; admission fee.)

Salou, by far the biggest resort on the Costa Dorada, has few pretensions. It is a well-ordered, no-frills playground for north European package tourists, offering them extensive beaches and a good range of facilities and entertainment. Salou also has a huge theme park, **Port Aventura**, which promises a journey of adventure through exotic lands, plus all sorts of rides, restaurants and live entertainment. During the early evening in summer, crowds assemble to watch the town's **illuminated fountain**, which was designed by Carlos Buigas, perhaps best known for the famous 'Magic Fountains' in Barcelona.

Cambrils, Salou's more classy neighbour, is an attractive fishing port turned resort that has a long seafront and a charming oddity in its large fleet of *bous* – small boats that carry outsize lamps when they go out to fish at night. The fish caught by these vessels supply the many good restaurants along the waterfront.

Rice harvest on the Ebro Delta

The Ebro Delta

The **Ebro Delta** is the largest of Catalunya's wetlands and, after France's Camargue, the

Dunes of the Ebro Delta

most important aquatic environment in the western Mediterranean. It is a major breeding ground for waders, waterfowl and sea birds. Some 7,700 hectares (19,000 acres) of the delta wetlands have been set aside as a protected National Park, making this a true birdwatcher's paradise. The tourist office at **Deltebre** can supply general information, maps, and details of boat excursions and birdwatching sites. Non-birdwatchers can enjoy the wide open spaces, the glittering green rice paddies (the basic ingredient for *paella* is grown here) and glimpses of the sleepy rural lifestyle.

Tortosa held a key strategic role for centuries as the last major town before the sea. Guarding the Ebro river, the **La Zuda** fortress at the top of the town was constructed by the Moors. Later it became a royal residence of the Aragónese kings. The **cathedral** in the old town was built between the 14th and 16th centuries, and is a fine example of Catalan Gothic architecture.

Picturesque Peñíscola

The Costa del Azahar

From the Ebro Delta to Valencia, the 'Orange Blossom Coast' begins south of the Tarragona provincial border and stretches for 100km (60 miles) down a section of coast that is well endowed with beaches backed by olive orchards and the citrus groves after which the coast is named.

➤ **Peñíscola**, picturesque and crowned by a medieval castle, is built on a rocky promontory. The **castle** (open: daily 9.30am–1pm and 3.15–6pm, summer 9.30am–9.30pm; admission fee) built by the Knights Templar on the ruins of a Moorish fortress, has two claims to fame: Pope Benedict XIII found asylum here after being dismissed from his position until his death in 1423; and it featured in the film *El Cid*, starring Charlton Heston. There's a museum and terrific sea views from the restored ramparts.

Sagunto (Roman Saguntum) underwent a nine-month siege by the Carthaginian general Hannibal in 219BC that ignited the Second Punic War. The inhabitants set fire to the city and themselves to avoid capture, but when Saguntum was eventually retaken, the Romans redeveloped it on a grand scale. Today, Sagunto's principal Roman monument is the heavily restored 2nd-century **amphitheatre**, where plays are performed during the summer. Nearby is a modest **archaeological museum** with Iberian, Roman and medieval relics. From the hilltop acropolis, **Castell de Sagunt**, there are sweeping views over the citrus orchards to the sea.

Valencia

Founded by the Romans in 138BC, Valencia later prospered as the capital of a far-flung Moorish kingdom until El Cid briefly recaptured it at the end of the 11th century. In 1238 Jaime I, El Conquistador (whose banner and sword can be seen in the **Museo Historico Municipal**), finally reconquered the city and proclaimed the Kingdom of Valencia. Today, Valencia is Spain's third largest city and most of its monuments are within the area bounded by the Turia Gardens (once a river) and the railway station.

The **cathedral** (open: 7.15am–1pm, 4.30–6.30pm) was started in 1262 on the site of a Moorish mosque but it is a mix of styles, with most parts dating from the 14th and the 15th centuries. Its octagonal Gothic bell tower, known as **El Micalet**, is a symbol of the city, and if you climb the 207 steps the view from the top is spectacular. A chapel contains what is said to be the Holy Grail.

Valencia's medieval Serrano Tower

Valencia is surrounded by more than 930 hectares (2,300 acres) of irrigated land *(huerta)* and for over 1,000 years disputes have been settled by the Tribunal de Aguas (Water Council). This is a group of eight men who meet every Thursday at midday outside the Door of the Apostles of the cathedral. Business is conducted verbally in Valenciano (the local language) with all decisions being final.

Valencia's **La Lonja** (Silk Exchange; open: Tues–Sat 9.15am–2pm and 4.30–8pm; Sun 9.30am–2pm; free) dates from the late 15th century. Besides being one of the finest secular Gothic structures in Europe it is also famous for its **Hall of Pillars** where finely crafted helicoidal columns curve graciously to the roof. Across the street the Modernist-style **central market** (open: daily until around 2pm), built between 1910 and 1926, is an irregular eight-sided iron girder and glass building where you will find an enticing array of meat, fish, vegetables and fruit. Outside, look for stalls that sell *paella* pans in a huge range of sizes.

Of Valencia's museums, **Museo Nacional de Cerámica** (open: Tues–Sat 10am–2pm, 4–8pm; Sun 10am–2pm; admission fee), housed in the astonishing Palacio del Marqués de Dos Aguas, is a gem and among its treasures it has hundreds of glorious glazed tiles *(azulejos)* for which the city is famous. The city's major art collection, at the **Museo de Bellas Artes** (open: Tues–Sat 9am–3pm; Sun 10am–2pm; free), has paintings by Bosch, El Greco, Goya and Velázquez, and a definitive collection of 15th-century Valencian art.

Valencian tiles

The **Serrano** and **Quart** towers are formidable reminders that such defensive fortifications were vital in centuries past. Just outside the city centre, Valencian architecture is entering the modern age via the city's new **Ciudad de las Artes y las Ciencias** (Arts and Sciences Park). The sprawling complex of futuristic buildings and parklands on the southern edge of the city is dedicated to fun and learning. **L'Hemisfèric** (screenings daily), an IMAX cinema and planetarium built in the shape of a gigantic open eye, was designed by Valencian architect Santiago Calatrava. Other attractions are the **Palacio de las Artes**, a concert hall with a huge open-air auditorium, the interactive exhibits at the **Museo de las Ciencias** (Science Museum), also designed by Calatrava, and the **Parque Oceanográfico**, an underwater city and aquarium with killer whales and dolphins.

> Artists and craftsmen work all year to create the elaborate *ninots* – papier-mâché figures that are set alight at the climax of Valencia's Las Fallas festival in March. Those figures voted too good for burning are saved from the flames and exhibited in the Museu Faller.

The Costa Blanca

The Costa Blanca, which begins to the south of Valencia, was named Akra Leuka ('White Headland') by ancient Greek tradesmen who founded a colony here 2,500 years ago. The hot, dry climate, brilliant light and miles of fine, sandy beaches and temperate water make the 'White Coast' one of Spain's liveliest tourist zones.

A town in two parts, **Gandia** has a busy resort on a vast beach down on the coast and a splendid 14th-century palace tucked away in its inland town centre. Birthplace of Duke Francisco de Borja, 16th-century noble turned Jesuit priest, the

Palacio de los Duques is now a showcase for splendid tapestries, paintings and antiques, many of them amassed by the pious duke.

Beyond Gandia, the town of **Dénia** is named after a Roman temple dedicated to the goddess Diana. Further south, the family resort of **Jávea** (Xàbia) has a fine beach and a pleasant old quarter. **Calpe** (Calp) is a former fishing village with pleasant sandy beaches in the lee of the **Peñón de Ifach**, an imposing volcanic outcrop. **Altea's** old houses climb steeply to a carefully preserved old quarter, little changed in the face of the tourist tide, and home to a thriving artistic community.

Benidorm used to symbolise the worst excesses of package tourism. It has a towering skyline that stretches far back from the 7-km (4-mile) beach, and provides what holiday makers want – sunshine, beaches, bars and entertainment. Surprisingly, the old fishermen's quarter still exists, a major saving grace. Likewise, there are sweeping views from the attractive **Balcón de Mer**, encompassing the town's crescent of beaches backed by the wind-sculpted mountains. Boats visit the **Isla de Benidorm**, an offshore bird sanctuary. Adding to its attractions, the **Terra Mitica** theme park has

Castell de Guadalest

opened south of Benidorm. With its state-of-the-art technology, visitors are taken on a journey through the history of the lost ancient civilisations of the Mediterranean, including Egypt, Greece, Rome and Iberia.

The Moorish eagles' nest village-fortress **Castell de Guadalest**, situated 28km (17 miles) northwest, is another favourite excursion.

Along Alicante's promenade

Alicante (Alicant), with a population of over a quarter of a million, is a bustling Mediterranean port with a splendid palm-lined **promenade**, lots of outdoor cafés and the spacious beach of **Playa Postiguet**. Alicante's imposing clifftop **Castillo de Santa Bárbara** was built on the site of a Carthaginian fort founded in the 3rd century BC. Below the castle, the old **Barrio de Cruz** is atmospheric and full of character. Here you will find the baroque façade of the 14th-century church of **Santa María** next to the **Museo de Arte de Siglo XX** (Museum of 20th-Century Art), focusing on the Spanish artists Miró, Picasso and Dalí.

Elche (Elx), situated a little way inland, is famous for its palm plantations, the largest in Europe. The **Palacio de Altamira**, a former royal holiday residence, is now occupied by an archaeological museum that has a replica of the famous *Dama de Elche* sculpture, which dates from the 5th century BC (the original is in Madrid).

Costa Cálida

The most famous stretch of the Costa Cálida (the 'Warm Coast'), which forms the southern portion of the Costa Blanca, is the **Mar Menor** (Little Sea), a vast lagoon almost completely sheltered from the Mediterranean by a 22-km (14-mile) spit. High-rise resort facilities have multiplied on the sandy breakwater, La Manga.

Cartagena, named after the Carthaginians, is an important port and naval base with a well-protected harbour overlooked by the ruins of the 14th-century **Castillo de la Concepción**. It is worth driving up for the views.

Almería's ramparts

Murcia, the inland capital of the province of the same name, which includes the Costa Cálida, is pleasant and prosperous, with a pretty old town. The 14th-century **Catedral de Santa María** is one of Spain's finest, adorned with a fabulous baroque façade. The Vélez chapel is a highlight of the interior, and in the museum there are wood sculptures by Francisco Salzillo (1707–83), Murcia's greatest artist. There are more of his works in the **Museo Salzillo**. Of Murcia's other museums, the **Museo Provincial de Bellas Artes** (Fine Arts) is the best.

The Costa de Almería

Almería is a modern city that reveals its Moorish origins in the form of the gigantic 8th-century **Alcazaba fortress**, which overhangs the town and port. The city's crenellated outer walls and a section of the turreted ramparts remain standing among the 35 hectares (87 acres) of ruins. The waterfront **Paseo de Almería** is ideal for strolling and shopping. Inland from the harbour, the fortified Gothic **cathedral** was completed in the mid-16th century.

This is Spain's dustbowl – a parched corner of the Mediterranean coast, where development has been kept at bay until very recently. On the coast are the growing resorts of **Mojácar**, **Roquetas de Mar** and **Garrucha**. Inland, the dramatic, desolate, desert-like landscape was a favourite with Western film-makers, who nicknamed it **Mini-Hollywood**.

Costa Tropical

The coastline of the province of Granada is the most attractive, and the least developed, part of Spain's southern coast. There are no large developments and few hotels; just numerous uncrowded small beaches with crystal clear water, surrounded by the mountains sloping down to the sea.

Motril sits in the midst of a fertile plain, while the hill of **Salobreña**, just west, is crowned with a magnificent castle. **Almuñécar** is the only other holiday resort of any size, and it has an ancient history. A fine aqueduct stands as a monument to the skills of the Roman engineers who constructed it during the reign of Antoninus Pius in the 2nd century AD.

The Costa del Sol

Nerja marks the eastern end of the Costa del Sol. Its cliff-top **Balcón de Europa** has a lovely palm-fringed promenade. The main attraction is the **Cueva de Nerja**, a truly cavernous grotto 4km (2½ miles) east of town. Wall paintings and archaeological finds indicate that the stalactite-encrusted cave – home to the world's longest stalactite at 59m (195ft) – has been inhabited since the days of Cro-Magnon man.

Málaga, by far the largest town, is the international gateway to the Costa del Sol, with many millions arriving at its airport every year. It also has a busy harbour overlooked by an **Alcazaba** (open: Tues–Sun Apr–Oct 9.30am–8pm; Nov–Mar 8.30am–7pm; admission fee) built by the Moors, now consisting mostly of landscaped ruins and home to a modest archaeological museum. At the top of the hill, the sprawling **Gibralfaro** fort ruins (open: daily 9.30am–8pm; free) afford spectacular views out to sea and inland to the mountains. A short distance from Málaga's grandiose but gloomy cathedral in the bustling pedestrianised commerical centre is the **Museo Picasso**. Some 200 of his paintings, drawings, sculptures and ceramics fill the 16th-century Buenavista Palace (open: Tues–Sun 10am–8pm, until 9pm at weekends; admission fee). Picasso was born nearby at Plaza de la Merced 15, which is now the **Museo Casa Natal** of the

Málaga's Plaza de la Constitución

Fundación Picasso. There is gallery space and the refurbished apartment where he was born.

Costumes and folk arts in the entertaining **Museo de Artes y Costumbres Populares** in a 17th-century inn near the Guadalmedina riverbed are worth a detour.

Torremolinos epitomises the popular side of the Costa del Sol, with tower-block hotels stretching well inland away from the famous **La Carihuela beach**, and its

Puerto Banús

chiringuitos – small beachside restaurants. So international is the resort that Spanish is almost a second language. The adjacent resort of **Fuengirola** is also popular, but more family-orientated.

Marbella, though, is the aristocrat of the Costa del Sol resorts, favoured by royalty and celebrities for decades. As a consequence, prices are higher here than anywhere else along the coast, but standards of accommodation and cuisine are superior, too. The 28-km (17-mile) beachfront is built up with expensive hotel complexes, and the spacious marina sees more than its fair share of luxury pleasure craft. Across the main road, the old town is an attractive warren of twisting streets and alleys full of shops, restaurants and the odd historic church.

Puerto Banús is Spain's answer to St Tropez. This chic 1970s marina-shopping-entertainment complex is full of tasteful bars, pricey boutiques, classy restaurants and nightclubs. Its waterfront parade is a catwalk for 'beautiful

Alleyway in Tarifa

people', many of whom arrive aboard the massive yachts that are berthed in the harbour.

Estepona, although quite small, is the last of the resorts on the western flank of the coast. It provides all the essentials for a sporty, modern vacation – large luxury hotels, beaches, golf courses and a marina – all in an engaging ambiance. Of Roman origin, Estepona preserves the remains of Moorish fortifications and watchtowers.

The Costa de la Luz

Stretching from the Straits of Gibraltar to the Portuguese border, the Atlantic-facing coast of southern Spain is aptly called the 'Coast of Light', because of the crystal clarity of its blue skies. Much loved by artists, it receives a mere trickle of tourists compared with its neighbour, the bustling Costa del Sol. It is extremely blustery and tourist facilities are limited, but to make up for that, there are long and uncrowded beaches, with easy access to Sevilla and to Spain's best national park, the Doñana *(see page 84)*.

Tarifa, the windsurfing capital of Europe, is just 13km (8 miles) across the water from North Africa. Morocco's Rif mountains hang on the horizon, and Tangier is often clearly visible. Accomplished windsurfers revel in the strong and consistently windy conditions prevailing at **Tarifa beach**.

Cádiz

The ancient city of **Cádiz**, isolated at the end of a very narrow peninsula of land running parallel to the coast, was founded by the Phoenicians in 1100BC and is considered to be Spain's oldest town. In fact, the amazing amalgam of history is not readily apparent, with only the remains of the Roman theatre giving much evidence of its age. Cádiz was reconquered by Alfonso X in 1262, granted the Monopoly of Trade with Africa by the Catholic Monarchs in 1493, and Columbus departed from here on his second and fourth voyages, in 1493 and 1502. In the latter part of the 16th century, the city twice came under attack by enemy naval forces. Just over a century later, a period of prosperity ensued when the Casa de Contratación, the monopoly rights for trade with the Americas, was transferred from Sevilla by order of Felipe V in 1717. A century later, on 19 March 1812, and while under attack from Napoleon's forces, the national parliament met in the St Felipe Neri church and proclaimed the first Spanish parliament.

The excellent **Museo de Cádiz** exhibits Phoenician and Roman artefacts and paintings by Francisco Zurbarán, as well as local crafts. Overlooking the ocean, the baroque and classical **cathedral** gives evidence of an extended construction period between 1772 and 1838, and has a landmark dome that glitters like gold in the sunshine. (The artist Murillo fell fatally from a scaffold when painting an altarpiece in 1816). The curious and

In 1587, English privateer Sir Francis Drake attacked the Spanish Armada as it lay at anchor in the Bay of Cádiz. Seizing some ships and burning others, he then razed the town before rampaging up and down the coast. His laconic comment, history records, was that he had 'singed the beard of the King of Spain'.

> ## Doñana National Park
>
> The largest and best known of Spain's national parks, this wild conservation zone, occupying the right bank of the Guadalquivir River at its estuary on the Atlantic Ocean, is the last great lowland wilderness in southern Europe. Covering some 75,000 hectares (185,000 acres), it has three distinct kinds of ecosystem: the *marismas* (salt marshes), the *matorral* (brushwood) and *las dunas* (the sand dunes). Within its boundaries can be found an amazing array of animal, bird and plant life, but what you see depends very much on the time of year. The best way see the park is by bus tour from the visitor centre at **El Acebuche**, tel: 959 448 711. Be warned, though, that this is a bumpy and rough ride.

unusual **Oratorio de la Santa Cueva** has underground chapels dating from 1783. Of more interest is the domed upper chapel added in 1796. Five spectacular paintings adorn its ceiling – three are fine examples of Goya's work.

Sanlúcar de Barrameda
Situated at the mouth of the Guadalquivir River on the Atlantic coast, Sanlúcar is a popular getaway for families from Sevilla. The town is also famed for vineyards that produce the grapes for *manzanilla*, a dry fino-style sherry. The sea breezes are said to supply *manzanilla*'s distinctive salty tang.

THE COSTA VERDE

Most people have an image of Spain as a land of white sun-baked villages, bullfights and swirling flamenco dancers. However, there exists a very different Spain in the north: Cantabria, Asturias and Galicia constitute a land of fishermen and farmers, where frequent and heavy rainfall makes for a verdant landscape.

Cantabria

There is plenty of variety in the autonomous region of Cantabria, where the sea and the snow-capped heights of the Picos de Europa can both be covered in a day's excursion. As well as fishing villages, ports and miles of undeveloped wilderness, the coast of Cantabria also offers several popular summer resorts, such as **Castro Urdiales**, **Laredo** and **Comillas**.

Santander, the capital of the region, successfully combines the roles of major port and tasteful resort, and the beach suburb of **El Sardinero**, with its flower gardens and numerous seafood bars, contributes to the city's holiday atmosphere. Overlooking the sea from the rugged peninsula is the Victorian-style **Magdalena Palace**, built for Alfonso XIII as a summer escape, a building of many architectural eccentricities. The **Museo Marítimo** (open: Tues–Sat 10am–9pm, 6pm Oct–Apr; admission fee) near the port is worth a visit.

Santillana del Mar, 26km (16 miles) west of Santander, is a perfectly preserved medieval village of gold-coloured stone houses, cobbled streets, farmyards and patrician mansions. The writer Jean-Paul Sartre described it as 'the prettiest village in Spain'. At the north end of the village is the **Colegiata** (Collegiate Church), dedicated to St Juliana

Picos de Europa

> **Altamira, 2km (1½ miles) inland from Santillana, is a cave complex dating from about 12,000BC that contains some of the finest prehistoric works of art in Europe. The caves are closed to the public to prevent further damage to the murals, but there is a museum containing faithful replicas and the 30,000-year-old remains of a caveman.**

(Santillana is a contraction of her name) whose tomb is inside. Its 12th-century Romanesque cloister is a gem. In the convent at the other end of the village, the **Museo Diocesano** specialises in carvings of saints and angels from nearby churches.

The **Picos de Europa**, just 25km (16 miles) from the coast, form part of the wall of the Cantabrian Mountains (Cordillera Cantábrica) that rise to a height of 2,600m (8,530ft). The N621 cuts through the dramatic **Desfiladero de la Hermida** gorge along the River Deva to **Potes**, the main gateway to the eastern Picos. Here you will find fine hiking country, fantastic scenery and good bird-watching. Don't forget to taste some *cabrales* – the pungent local blue cheese.

Asturias

Asturias is a wild, rugged province known for its fiercely independent people and potent cider. They say that this is the true Spain, because it was the only corner of the country that did not succumb to the Moors when they overran the rest of the peninsula in the 8th century. A band of Christian soldiers, led by local hero Pelayo, descended from the mountains and initiated the Reconquest with a small but significant victory over the Moors at the Battle of Covadonga in 722. A modern statue of Pelayo stands in the main square of **Covadonga**, and his remains are interred in the **Santa Cueva** (Holy Cave), where he saw a vision of the Virgin Mary that inspired his victory – now a place of pilgrimage.

Oviedo

The Asturian capital is outwardly nondescript, but Oviedo's compact historic centre has some fine monuments, plus a host of friendly *sidrarías*, bars serving the local cider *(sidra)*. The **cathedral** culminates in a flourish with a tall and elaborate Gothic tower, and its Cámara Santa (Holy Chamber) is a shrine built by Alfonso II to preserve holy relics brought from Toledo after it fell to the Moors. Behind the cathedral, the **Museo Arqueológico** is housed in a splendid old palace-convent with a gorgeous plateresque cloister. Beyond the city centre, you will find three remarkable examples of pre-Romanesque architecture. A short walk to the northeast is **San Julián de los Prados**. On the wooded slopes 3km (2 miles) northwest of Oviedo, is **Santa María del Naranco**. The greatest of the Asturian churches, it was designed as the main reception hall of a palace built for Ramiro I in 842. Just up the hill, part of the former palace chapel, **San Miguel de Lillo**, has beautiful Byzantine-style carvings.

Galicia

Galicia is an autonomous region in the northwestern corner of the Iberian Peninsula, with its own language, *Gallego*. It is made up of the four provinces of A Coruña, Lugo, Ourense and Pontevedra. Rugged and isolated, its coastline is characterised by narrow, rocky *rías* (sea inlets) battered by the Atlantic.

San Miguel de Lillo, Oviedo

Pilgrims to the shrine of St James, Santiago de Compostela

Galicia's scalloped coastline is perfect for boating, fishing and, when the sun does shine, swimming. Although the Atlantic coast south from La Coruña has the more spectacular *rías*, the northern indentations, the **Rías Altas**, has several unspoiled resort towns and quiet beaches. The medieval village of **Pont- edeume** is an old-fashioned resort with a long sandy beach. **Ortigueira** is noted for its fine beach and lush hills. **El Barqueiro**, a pic- turesque fishing village, has a white sand beach, and **Viveiro's** monuments offer a contrast to the fishing port and resort ambience. Popular with bathers and fishermen, **Foz** has a particularly mild microclimate.

La Coruña

The capital of the region and Spain's second largest port, **La Coruña** (A Coruña in Galician) is worth a visit for its historic old town and unusual beach. It possesses Spain's oldest light- house, the **Torre de Hércules**, said to be the only Roman light- house still in operation. Now clad in an 18th-century shell, it affords splendid Atlantic vistas from the lookout 242 steps above ground. The Spanish Armada sailed for England, and to defeat, from La Coruña's busy port in 1588. Behind the port, **Avenida de la Marina** curves east to the old town and its fa- mous *galerias* (glassed-in terraces) and historic churches and monasteries. The 16th-century **Castillo de San Antón**, guard- ing the harbour approaches, houses an archaeological museum.

Santiago de Compostela

Santiago is the third holiest shrine in Christendom (after Jerusalem and Rome). Its claim to fame originates from 813, when brilliant stars attracted a peasant called Pelayo to a field where the tomb of the Apostle St James (Santiago in Spanish) was revealed to him. Since then pilgrims from all over Europe have travelled the **Camino de Santiago** (Pilgrim Way) across northern Spain to this remote corner of the country, at one time the western boundary of the known world. In 1189 Alexander III decreed it a Holy City – a status shared only by Rome and Jerusalem. It is also a lively and attractive place with beautiful buildings, colourful plazas, and a largely pedestrian heart, ideal for sightseeing and relaxing. Wherever you wander in Santiago de Compostela, you will be within sight of a historic church or monastery. There are

The Legend of St James

Unsubstantiated by the Bible, the legend of St James sprang up in the 9th century when a star is supposed to have directed some Galician shepherds to the Apostle's grave. The story goes that St James brought Christianity to Spain after the death of Christ. When he returned to Judaea, he was martyred by Herod, and his disciples fled with the body in a magical vessel with no sails or crew. It ferried them to the village of Padrón, and the body was buried nearby.

Its 'discovery' in the 9th century was hailed as a miracle, and there were several more to follow, including a ghostly sighting of St James on horseback slaying Moors by the thousand at the Battle of Clavijo in 844. These exploits earned him the title 'Matamoros' or Moor Slayer. It also elevated him to the position of patron saint of the Reconquest, and of Spain. The cult of St James spread far and wide, and by the end of the 11th century, the Pilgrim Way (Camino de Santiago) was attracting pilgrims from all over Europe.

also plenty of bars and restaurants serving delicious local seafood, especially *pulpo* (octopus) fresh from the *rías* (inlets).

Construction of the huge and magnificent **cathedral** (open: summer Mon–Sat 10am–2pm and 4–7.30pm, Sun 10am–2pm; winter Mon–Sat 10am–1.30pm and 4–6.30pm, Sun 10am–1.30pm; admission fee to museum and cloisters), replacing an earlier one built on the site where James's remains were found, began in 1075 but was not completed until 1128. Numerous additions and changes have taken place over the centuries, and in the 18th century the beautifully symmetrical double staircase and towers of the Obradoiro façade were completed.

Santiago de Compostela

Just inside the main entrance, the 800-year-old **Pórtico de la Gloria** (Door of Glory) is a marvel of Romanesque sculpture by the artist known simply as Master Mateo. A 13th-century polychrome **statue of St James** takes the spotlight on the main altar, which stands above the crypt where the saint's remains lie at rest. It's also impossible to miss the giant incense burner, the **botafumeiro**, so large that it takes several men to swing it, pendulum fashion, during ceremonial occasions.

At a right angle to the cathedral's entrance, on Plaza del Obradoiro, the **Hostal dos Reis Católicos** has a stupendous façade. Founded by Fernando and Isabel in 1499, as a pilgrim hostel, this is now a luxurious *parador (see page 177).* For an added insight into local customs, crafts and folklore, visit the **Museo do Pobo Galego** (open: Tues–Sat 10am–2pm and 4–8pm; Sun 11am–2pm; admission fee) housed in the old convent of **Santo Domingo**, which has triple helicoidal (spiral) staircases, without any supports, connecting all levels of the convent.

Pontevedra

A strategic port since the Middle Ages, this is one of Galicia's most charming towns, with many fine old buildings, gardens and spacious squares. The city's pride and joy is the plateresque **Iglesia de Santa María la Mayor** in the old fishermen's quarter. Its sculpted façade is divided into compartments, each telling a New Testament story.

The patron saint of Pontevedra, the Pilgrim Virgin, is commemorated in the curvaceous 18th-century **Iglesia de la Virgen de la Peregrina**. Nearby, the **Iglesia de San Francisco** was founded in the 14th century and the provincial museum, housed in interconnecting historic mansions, offers departments of archaeology and art, and some enlightening exhibits on the Galician seafaring way of life.

Bayona (Baiona)

Bayona was the first town in Spain to learn, on 1 March 1493, of Columbus's landing in the New World. Today the town is an attractive resort, largely undiscovered by mass tourism, although its beaches are small and tend to become crowded in season. A few miles out of the town lies the better and wider beach of **Playa de América**. Bayona's delightful fishing port is full of traditional houses and *tapas* bars. Set on a *ría*, the town overlooks a wooded promontory where an ancient castle has been transformed into a *parador*, with wonderful views.

A Basque farmer

THE BASQUE COUNTRY

The Spanish Basque Country, or País Vasco, is an autonomous region consisting of the three provinces of Alava, Guipúzoca and Vizcaya. Along with their cousins north of the border in France, around a quarter of the Basque people speak Euskara, a language unrelated to any other. They are fiercely independent of spirit and mind – so much so that the ongoing campaign for independence by the terrorist organisation ETA has cost many lives over the years. Riots and protests, with varying degrees of violence, can erupt very suddenly. On the other hand, this pretty and normally peaceful region, with many attractive towns, is considered to have the finest cuisine in Spain.

Vitoria

Vitoria (Gasteiz), the capital of the Alava province and region, was founded by Sancho the Wise, the Navarrese king, in 1181. In 1200 the town passed into the hands of Castile, later growing rich on the wool trade. The medieval town centre, laid out in a concentric pattern on the fortified hilltop, is home to the 14th-century **Catedral de Santa María**. Nearby, the **Museo Provincial de Arqueología** features Iron-Age and Roman relics. The prosperous merchants built gracious Renaissance mansions and fine churches such as **San Miguel** on **Plaza de la Virgen Blanco** (White Virgin Square) to the south. A monument here commemorates the Duke of Wellington's 1813 victory in the Wars of Independence. The city's spacious main square, **Plaza de España**, is a classic 18th-century Spanish ensemble, with the town hall on the north side.

San Sebastián

San Sebastián (Donostia), the capital of Guipúzoca province, is a beautiful city situated around the Bahía de la Concha (Shell Bay) – a semicircle of sandy beaches flanked by two peninsulas. Formerly a fishing and trading port, San Sebastián was elevated to the heights of favoured royal seaside resort in the mid-19th century. Having been mostly burnt to the ground on 13 August 1813, during the Wars of Independence, it has little by way of historical monuments, but it does have numerous *belle-époque* villas and buildings. A century later, another conflict, World War I, brought substantial changes to the city as Spain's position of neutrality and San Sebastián's proximity to

Bahía de la Concha, San Sebastián

France (the border is less than 15 miles away) made it a convenient haven for many wealthy people endeavouring to avoid the war. This influx transformed San Sebastián, and even now it has a much more well-healed ambiance than many Spanish towns.

The **Playa de la Concha** dominates the city and makes it a popular family resort. At one end, directly under **Monte Urgull**, are the colourful streets of the **Parte Vieja** (Old Quarter), radiating from the arcaded Plaza de la Constitución. The atmosphere still recalls something of an old-time fishing village, and the narrow streets are the focus for the early evening walkabout, when locals and visitors cram the multitude of bars and restaurants. The city's oldest church, **San Vicente**, is to be found in this area, as is the **Museo San Telmo**, which displays the municipal art collections and has sections on local history and crafts. Not far from the fishing port, from where there are summer-season boat trips to the **Isla de Santa Clara** in the bay, the church of **Santa María** has an ornate baroque façade. If you want to learn more about local seafaring traditions, including whaling, take a look around the aquarium at the end of the harbour.

Relaxing in Bilbao

Bilbao

Bilbao is the capital of Vizcaya province and was once the industrial heartland of the Basque Country. It is now reinventing itself and has a thriving central district with broad boulevards and leafy parks, a metro system designed by Norman Foster, and the historic **Casco Viejo** (Old Quarter).

Bilbao's Museo Guggenheim

Until recently the city had no real attractions to offer, but that changed in 1997 when the **Museo Guggenheim** (open: Tues–Sun 10am–8pm; admission fee), designed by California-based architect Frank Gehry, was inaugurated. This massive, futuristic structure, funded primarily by the Basque government, has become the symbol of Bilbao, its shimmering titanium roof rising dramatically beside the banks of the Nervión. Inside, 19 spacious galleries on three floors accommodate works predominantly from 1960 to the present day, including works from the Guggenheim collections of New York and Venice.

In addition, the **Museo de Bellas Artes** (Fine Arts Museum) is one of the country's best collections. It offers a rich survey of Spanish classics – El Greco, Goya, and an honest 'warts and all' portrait of Felipe IV by Velázquez – as well as Flemish and Italian masterpieces. The museum's upper floor is devoted to Basque and international 20th-century art.

CASTILLA Y LEÓN

This huge area north and west of Madrid is bordered by Portugal and the Cantabrian mountains behind the Costa Verde. An autonomous region with its capital at León, it consists of nine provinces: Ávila, Burgos, León, Palencia, Salamanca, Segovia, Soria, Valladolid and Zamora (Ávila and Segovia are covered in the Around Madrid section – *see pages 36 and 41*).

Burgos

> Founded in 884 as a stronghold against the Moors, **Burgos** succumbed to the invaders but was reconquered in 951 and became the capital of Castile, an honour that it held until 1492, when the Catholic Monarchs transferred their court to Valladolid. In 1812, during the War of Independence, Burgos, then a French garrison, was besieged by Wellington's troops. It was also prominent during the Spanish Civil War, when Franco was declared Head of State and Generalíssimo there in 1936. The city subsequently became the seat of the provisional government, and it was from La Isla Palace in Burgos, on 1 April 1939, that Franco proclaimed the ceasefire.

The city's most famous citizen, born in 1026, was

Burgos cathedral

Rodrigo Diaz, the soldier of fortune better known as El Cid *(see page 19)*, and his remains are interred in the **cathedral**, which is the third largest in Spain (after Sevilla and Toledo). This stunningly intricate Gothic jewel is also one of the most beautiful churches in the country. Construction began in 1221 but it took 400 years to complete, and it holds attractions

Equestrian statue of El Cid

that are classical, historical and even eccentric. Don't miss the splendid **Constable's chapel** behind the altar, the burial place of Hernández de Velasco, Constable of Castile during the reign of the Catholic Monarchs. Gil de Siloé's altar of St Anne is partnered by his son Diego's exquisite golden stairway, built in 1519; it now leads nowhere and is only used during the highly ceremonious Easter celebrations. Look out, also, for the **Papamoscas** (Flycatcher), a clown dating from the 15th century, who sits above a clock high to the left of the main door, and opens and closes his mouth at each stroke of the bell.

It's always fun to join the Burgalése on their evening stroll down the tree-lined Paseo del Espolón. This follows the banks of the normally placid River Arlanzón, passing the decorative, crenellated **Arco de Santa María**, once the main entrance to the city. At the end of the Paseo, **El Cid** greets you, in the form of an impressive equestrian statue. Nearby is the intricate and strange façade of the **Casa del Cordón** where, on 23 April 1497, Fernando and Isabel welcomed Columbus back from his second voyage to the New World. Back across the river, two noble Renaissance houses serve as the **Burgos Museum**.

The former Monasterio San Marco in León, now a *parador*

On the western outskirts of Burgos, the **Convento de las Huelgas** was founded in the 12th century. Behind fortress-like walls, the complex is something of an architectural hybrid, with Romanesque elements and a fine Mudéjar-Gothic cloister. Kings were crowned and buried here, and a small museum displays some of the ecclesiastical treasures and artworks amassed by the convent's powerful abbesses.

León

León was founded in AD68 by the Roman 7th Legion, who built their fortifications on the hill where the cathedral now stands. During the 4th century the Romans were forced out by the Visigoths who, in turn, were defeated by the Moors early in the 8th century. Located on the edge of the Moors' scope of influence, control of the city fluctuated. By the 10th century it had been repopulated by Mozarabs (Christian refugees from the south) and, as the seat of the Kingdom of León, was considered the most important Christian city in Spain. However, in 996 the Moors invaded again and it wasn't until the 11th century that the city was finally reconquered. During the 12th century its prominence began to diminish until, in 1235, it amalgamated with Castile. Today, León is a prosperous, modern city with a somewhat old-fashioned ambiance.

León's most impressive monument is the 13th-century **Catedral de Santa María de Regla** (open: June–Sept Mon–Sat 8.30am–1.30pm, 4–8pm, Sun 8.30am–2.30pm, 5–8pm; Oct–May until 7pm). Inspired by the Gothic cathedral at Chartres in France, it has the most glorious complement of stained glass in Spain – 125 huge windows and 57 smaller glassed areas dating from the 13th to the 20th centuries. The west façade sports mismatched towers and elaborately carved portals. Tours of the cloister, an elegant mix of Gothic and Renaissance elements, lead to the **Diocesan Museum**, with archaeological exhibits and both fine and applied arts.

A few streets west of the cathedral, an equestrian statue of St Isidoro crowns the south side of the **Colegiata de San Isidoro** (Collegiate Church). In the Moorish invasions, the saint's relics were evacuated to León from Sevilla, where he had been archbishop, and they attract pilgrims to this day. The **San Isidoro Museum** (guided visits: daily 10am–1.30pm and 4–6.30pm; closed Sun pm; Jul–Aug Mon–Sat 9am–8pm, Sun 9am–2pm) contains the **Panteón Real**, the burial place of 23 kings and queens and nine infantas. It also has magnificent frescoes in the 'Capilla Sixtina' ('the Sistine Chapel of Romanesque'), and a **Chapter Treasury Room**, where notable exhibits include chalices from the early Middle Ages.

Built in 1168 for the Knights of Santiago, and later used as a pilgrims' hospice, the former **Monasterio de San Marco** was rebuilt in the 16th century and has a magnificent plateresque façade. Today, it is one of Spain's finest *paradores*. The **Museo Arqueológico Provincial** is based in the cloister and sacristy of the adjacent church.

Salamanca

Hannibal made this his westernmost possession when he conquered this city in the 3rd century BC. Later, under the name of Helmántica, its strategic location helped it to

Salamanca and the Old Cathedral

become an important city in the Roman Empire. In 1102, after periods of rule by the Visigoths and Moors, Salamanca was reconquered by the forces of Alfonso VI. In 1218, Alfonso IX founded the first university in Spain here, and it soon gained an international reputation. Between the 15th and early 18th centuries Salamanca was the main cultural centre of the Spanish Empire. It suffered badly during the War of Independence, and it was entered by Wellington in the summer of 1812, just before the Battle of Salamanca. The cultural importance of the city has been recognised by UNESCO, which has declared it a World Heritage Site.

The social hub of Salamanca is the graceful **Plaza Mayor**, considered to be the most perfect plaza in Spain, begun in 1729 during the reign of Felipe V. The street-level arcades, illuminated by delightful lanterns, support three additional storeys and the most prominent buildings are the Town Hall and Royal Pavilion.

Salamanca has two connected, and very contrasting, cathedrals. The **Catedral Vieja** (Old Cathedral; open Apr–Sept: daily 10am–1.30pm and 4–7.30pm; Oct–Mar: daily 10am–12.30pm and 4–5.30pm; admission fee) was begun in 1114, finished a century later, and is one of the most important Romanesque structures in the country. It has a remarkable, highly intricate 15th-century altar sculpted by the Italian, Nicolás Florentino. Look, also, for an altarpiece featuring a fine 12th-century statue known as the *Virgen de la Vega* and the unusual Mudéjar dome in the **Capilla de Talavera**. Construction of the **Catedral Nueva** (New Cathedral; open Apr–Sept: daily 10am–2pm and 4–8pm; Oct–Mar: daily 10am–1pm, 4–6pm; free) began in 1513 as the old one was too small, and although it has Renaissance and baroque additions, it is considered to be one of the last Gothic structures built in Spain. Inside, the triple-naved cathedral has fine baroque choir stalls and 18 side chapels, of which the most notable is the **Capilla Dorada** (Golden Chapel), with 110 sculptures. The **Diocesan Museum** in the old chapter house has a notable collection of paintings by Fernando Gallego, an underrated master of 15th-century Hispano-Flemish style.

Salamanca's **university**, founded in 1218, was one of the greatest centres of learning in medieval Europe. The 16th-century plateresque façade of the main building is highly intricate, and the lecture halls around the central patio illustrate centuries of architectural and decorative detail. Nearby, the **Patio de las Escuelas** is surrounded by plateresque buildings.

Salamanca has many other attractions, including some interesting convents, the **Salamanca Museum**, the circular Romanesque **Iglesia de San Marcos** (dating from 1178) and the very unusual **Casa de las Conchas** (House of Shells), built by a Knight of Santiago who decorated the exterior with hundreds of carved scallop-shells, the symbol of the pilgrimage to Santiago de Compostela.

Around Salamanca

➤ **La Alberca**, the principal town of the pretty mountain region of the Sierra de la Peña de Francia, is Old Spain personified: narrow alleys are lined with simple whitewashed homes, their delicate wooden balconies weighed down by flowerpots. The highlight of the local calendar is the Feast of the Assumption (15 August), when the entire population turns out to celebrate in traditional costume.

You can walk all the way around the hill town of **Ciudad Rodrigo** in no time. Take the 2-km (1½-mile) path that follows the medieval defences past the old castle (now a *parador)*. There are about a dozen worthy old mansions in town, most with interesting stone carvings and inviting patios. The Plaza Mayor is distinguished by the **Casa Consistoral** (Town Hall), a 16th-century arcaded palace with a belfry. The exterior of the **cathedral** is covered with fine sculptural details, and still bears the marks of shellfire from a famous battle during the War of Independence, when the Duke of Wellington captured the town from French forces.

Soria

The smallest provincial capital of Spain spreads along a poplar-shaded bend of the River Duero and typifies Old Castile. The small chapel of the **Ermita de la Soledad** contains a treasured 16th-century wooden statue of Christ. Across the street, the **Museo Numantino** specialises in relics found in the Roman ruins just north of town. Soria has an impressive collection of churches, all in toast-coloured stone and almost all dating from the 12th century. They include: **Santo Domingo**, with its Romanesque façade; **San Juan de Rabanera**, with Byzantine touches and a hint of early Gothic; and the **Co-catedral de San Pedro**, with a plateresque portal and a Romanesque cloister. On the left bank of the river, **San Juan de Duero** used to be a monastery of the Knights Templar.

Elaborate façades in Valladolid

Valladolid

Valladolid may be less beautiful than other cities in the region, but it has more than its fair share of history and attractions. It was the home and birthplace of Castilian kings between the 12th and 17th centuries – including Felipe II and Felipe IV; capital of the empire during the reigns of Felipe II and Felipe III; the place where Fernando wed Isabel in 1469, thus marrying the kingdoms of Aragón, Catalunya, Naples, Castile and León into a united Spain; home to Cervantes and Christopher Columbus; and, in 1809, headquarters for Napoleon.

Valladolid is one of the hotbeds of the Isabelline style – a form of overblown plateresque expressed in extravagant, florid ornamentation and named after Isabel of Castile. A perfect example of this style is the unusually elaborate façade of the **Colegio de San Gregorio**, founded in the late 15th century by Fray Alonso de Burgos, Confessor to Queen Isabella. The college has housed, since 1933, the **Museo**

Nacional de Escultura (National Museum of Sculpture), the 'Prado' of religious statuary, with works ranging from the 13th to the 18th centuries. The star here is the woodcarving genius of the Spanish Renaissance, Alonso Berruguete, said to have studied under Michelangelo.

The focal point for the city is the massive **statue of Christ** that stands tall on its pinnacle atop the cathedral. Commissioned by Felipe II in the late 16th century, it was designed and started by Juan de Herrera, co-creator of Felipe II's Escorial complex, but completed much later, which accounts for its stylistic complexity. Inside, the highlight is the altarpiece by Juan de Juni, an Italian-trained Frenchman of the mid-16th century, and one of Juan de Arfe's monstrances, dating from 1587, can be seen in the museum.

On 19 May 1506 Christopher Columbus, by then a broken man, died in the arcaded two-storey building that is now the **Casa-Museo de Colón** (House-Museum of Columbus). It displays relics and documents relating to the Age of Discovery. The **Casa de Cervantes** commemorates Miguel Cervantes, creator of *Don Quixote*, who lived here for several years. The **Oriental Museum**, adjoining the massive edifice of the 18th-century **Royal College of the Augustinian Fathers**, has one of the best collections of its kind in Spain.

Castles of Castilla

In Castilla it is only natural to expect to see castles, and two of the best examples can be found close to Valladolid. **Coca Castle**, 63km (39 miles) south of of the city is a late 15th-century masterpiece of Spanish Mudéjar military design, strongly influenced by Islamic architecture. And **Peñafiel Castle**, 35km (22 miles) east of Valladolid is more than 200m (656ft) long but less than 25m (80ft) across, and sits stranded high on a lonely hilltop.

Coca Castle, a masterpiece of military design

Zamora

A strategic walled stronghold above the right bank of the River Duero, the often besieged city of Zamora changed hands many times in the centuries of the Reconquest. To get the finest view of this appealing historic city, cross the Duero by the 14th-century bridge. From the south bank, you can admire the Byzantine cupola of the **cathedral**, built in the 12th century and roofed in curved stone tiles laid like fish scales. Its interior features a fine altarpiece by Fernando Gallego.

East of Zamora, the medieval hilltop town of **Toro** is a national monument. Besides some splendid Romanesque churches, convents and mansions, and a ruined 10th-century castle, Toro's greatest pride is the **Iglesia Colegiata de Santa María la Mayor** (Collegiate Church of St Mary the Great). A Romanesque classic, it houses a most unusual 16th-century painting entitled *The Virgin and the Fly*, which is widely considered to be a faithful portrait of Isabel of Castile.

NAVARRA AND LA RIOJA

Pamplona

Moving from west to east, the Pyrenees gain altitude, and the Basque character of the countryside and the people recedes. Navarra once extended into France, but the mountains now form a natural border between France and Spain. In fact, it is not a region that is much frequented by visitors, except at one time of the year, when they flock to **Pamplona** (Iruña) for the world-famous Fiesta de San Fermín (Festival of St Fermin), immortalised by Ernest Hemingway, which begins on 7 July every year.

At this time the city is swamped by tens of thousands of people in festive mood. The early morning *encierros* (running of the bulls) that are a prelude to the afternoon *corridas* (bullfights) are most famous, but, in fact, this fiesta has

---

The Running of the Bulls

Pamplona's Fiesta de San Fermín (Festival of St Fermin), specifically the *encierros* or 'running of the bulls', so entranced the writer Ernest Hemingway that he immortalised it in his novel *The Sun Also Rises* (1926). Since then, the fiesta has become an international crowd-puller, and the *encierros* are just part of the celebrations, which run the gamut from wood-chopping contests to fireworks.

The *encierros* take place daily from 7 to 12 July. At 8am when the bulls are released, serious *corredores* (runners), usually dressed in white with red sashes, attempt to run for a few steps, at least, side-by-side with the bulls along the route to the Plaza de Toros (bullring), while the main crowd are just happy to avoid the bulls if they can. Exciting it may be, but participants are regularly maimed and killed. Hemingway, known locally as Don Ernesto, is commemorated by a bust that stands just outside the bullring.

many other planned surprises, including a huge fireworks display every night – and many impromptu ones.

Visiting Pamplona at any other time of the year, you should see the **cathedral**, with its magnificent cloister, and explore the narrow and colourful streets of the former Jewish quarter, south and west of the café-lined **Plaza del Castillo**.

Pamplona's Café Iruña on the central Plaza del Castillo

Logroño

Logroño in La Rioja is the lively capital of Spain's premier wine region. Among medieval pilgrim travellers, the province of La Rioja was renowned for cheerful and attentive hospitality. Their first stop would have been **Santa María de Palacio**, dating from the 11th century and topped by a tall, graceful, pyramidal tower. The considerably younger **cathedral**, a few streets to the south of the church, features a generously sculpted main portal. Behind the cathedral lie the atmospheric narrow streets of the old town.

ARAGÓN

The modern, autonomous community of Aragón is approximately coextensive with the historic Kingdom of Aragón, and encompasses the three provinces of Huesca, Zaragoza and Teruel, extending south from the Pyrenees.

Huesca

The rugged northern section of this province is a sparsely populated and visually striking region that really is

Ordesa National Park

'undiscovered' Spain. The tallest peaks of all the Pyrenees belong to Aragón, and there are several good ski resorts in Astún, Candanchú and Formigal.

Jaca, the gateway to the Aragón Pyrenees and an old stop on the Pilgrim Way, has been of great military significance for at least 12 centuries, ever since it figured in one of the earliest victories over the Moors. The enormous, low-lying 16th-century **fortress** at the edge of town is a symbol of its former strategic importance. Its other notable monument is the **cathedral**, which dates from the 11th century and is one of the oldest in Spain. Among the highlights are the fine Romanesque frescoes, Renaissance sculptures and a plateresque altarpiece.

➤ **Ordesa National Park**, reckoned to be one of Europe's best-kept secrets, is a spectacular mountain park accessible from the village of **Torla** 60km (37 miles) northeast of Jaca. Pyrenean chamois perch on the cliffs here, as do roe deer, wild boar, and the last surviving herd of ibex (mountain goats with backward curving horns) in the Pyrenees. In the Ordesa Valley dramatic canyon walls, 1,000m (3,250ft) in height, are cloaked in ancient beech, silver fir and mountain pine forests. In summer the park can be busy, but snow prevents access from October to April.

Zaragoza

Capital of Aragón and the region's one big town, **Zaragoza**
can trace its origins back to the Iberians. In 19BC the Romans
founded the city of Caesaraugusta. Subsequently, the Moors
held the city for 400 years until Alfonso I (The Fighter) reconquered it in 1118.

The long, narrow **Plaza del Pilar** is the social centre of
Zaragoza, and is home to magnificent monuments and modern fountains. Of the monuments, the cathedral-basilica of
Nuestra Señora del Pilar (Our Lady of the Pillar), the
largest and most important, is located in the centre. According to tradition, the Virgin Mary appeared here in AD40,
standing on the jasper column that forms part of the elaborate **Capilla del Pilar**. The cathedral's superb main altarpiece is the work of the sculptor Damián Forment.
Zaragoza's other cathedral, **La Seo**, was built in the 12th
century. Although the cathedral is mainly Gothic, it features
Romanesque remnants, Mudéjar decorations and striking
baroque postscripts, plus a 17th-century belfry displaying
one of the finest tapestry collections in Spain. The **Museo
del Foro de Caesaraugusta**
(open: Tues–Sat 10am–2pm,
5–8pm, Sun 10am–2pm) al-
lows visitors to see the
remains of the city's 1st-
century Roman forum.

Between the two cathe-
drals is **La Lonja**, considered
the finest example of civil architecture in Zaragoza and
constructed as an exchange
between 1541 and 1551.

To the west of the city
centre, the restored Moorish

**Nuestra Señora del Pilar,
Zaragoza**

Teruel's Mudéjar-style Torre San Martín

Aljafería Palace was founded in the 11th century, then adapted by the Christian kings of Aragón after the Reconquest. Across the moat (now a sunken garden) you enter the world of Muslim Spain. Part of the palace now serves as Aragón's parliament.

Teruel

The capital of Lower Aragón, **Teruel** is a prime showcase for Mudéjar-style architecture. When Alfonso II of Aragón captured the town from the Moors in 1171, most Muslims chose to stay until their enforced expulsion at the end of the 15th century. This was time enough for the creation of lasting works of Mudéjar art.

The **cathedral's** Mudéjar elements include the finely decorated 13th-century brick tower and the lantern in the dome. Two other local towers are considered to be classics of the style: the **Torre San Martín** and **Torre del Salvador**.

The Gothic **Iglesia de San Pedro** (St Peter's Church) has a 13th-century Mudéjar tower. Adjoining the church is a chapel containing the mausoleum of the **Lovers of Teruel**, a star-crossed 13th-century couple whose tale of love lost and early death has inspired generations of Spanish writers.

CASTILLA-LA MANCHA

This is a geographically diverse area that wraps around Madrid to the east and south and consists of the provinces of Albacete, Ciudad Real, Cuenca, Guadalajara and Toledo (the latter is covered in Around Madrid – *see page 33*).

La Mancha

The vast, parched plain of La Mancha, with its endless, shimmering horizons, was the perfect setting for the adventures of author Miguel Cervantes' myopic, idealistic knight, Don Quixote, and his squire, Sancho Panza. The names of several of La Mancha's villages and towns appear in the text of *Don Quixote de la Mancha*, none more important than **El Toboso** (in Toledo province), the home of Dulcinea, the woman of Quixote's dreams. Dulcinea's house is open to the public.

Miguel de Cervantes Saavedra

Cervantes was born on the very edge of La Mancha, at **Alcalá de Henares**, in 1547. The son of an itinerant doctor, his education was minimal. He travelled, became a soldier and was wounded in the naval Battle of Lepanto in 1571. Four years later he was captured by corsairs and held in Algiers for five years before being ransomed. It is said he wrote the first draft of *Don Quixote* in prison at **Argamasilla de Alba** (northwest of Almagro). It was published in 1605 to great acclaim, and has been translated into more languages than any other book except the Bible. A second part appeared in 1615, a year before his death.

Hillside houses of Cuenca

Cuenca

Cuenca, away from the main highways in the foothills of the
Sistema Iberico range in eastern Castilla-La Mancha, is not
to be missed. The old town occupies a dramatic site perched
on a precipice above the rivers Huécar and Júcar. It is here
that Cuenca's famous medieval **Casas Colgadas** (Hanging
Houses) literally hang out over the precipice void.

The **Museo de Arte Abstracto Español**, housed within
the Casas Colgadas, has a collection of outstanding contemporary Spanish paintings and sculptures, and the nearby
Museo de Cuenca, a provincial archaeological museum,
occupies a 14th-century palace, La Casa del Curato. The
cathedral is a unique 12th-century Gothic/Anglo-Norman
structure that underwent significant renovations in the 17th
century. Its interior is very plain but the treasures here include a 14th-century Byzantine diptych embellished with
precious stones, unique in Spain.

Sigüenza

Sigüenza, northwest of the unexciting capital, Guadalajara, is home to a classic fortress and an outsized **Plaza Mayor**, one of the most beautiful main squares in Spain. Founded by Visigoths and occupied by Moors, Sigüenza's fort was reconquered by Christian forces early in the 12th century. It became the headquarters of the bishops of Sigüenza, housing around 1,000 soldiers and more than 300 horses during the 15th century. Today, it is a *parador*. At first sight, the crenellated **cathedral** also resembles a fortress. It contains a famous sculpture, the **sepulchre of 'El Doncel'** ('The Page'). Commissioned by Queen Isabel, it honours a young servant killed fighting in Granada in 1486. Opposite, the **Museo Diocesano de Arte** packs its 14 halls with everything from prehistoric axes to an ethereal rendering of the Virgin by Zurbarán.

EXTREMADURA

Lying to the southwest of Madrid, Extremadura is bordered to the north by the province of Salamanca, to the east by the region of Castilla-La Mancha, to the west by Portugal and to the south by Andalucía. It consists of the two provinces of Cáceres and Badajoz, and is one of the least-visited regions of Spain. Extremadura reached a brief zenith during Roman times, when a provincial capital was established at Mérida, but its real fame comes from being the 'Cradle of the Conquistadores' – adventurers such as Hernando Pizarro and Diego García, who colonised the Americas in the 16th century and brought back great riches to Spain.

Cáceres

Cáceres was founded in 34BC by the Romans, who named it Norba Caesarina. Having declined after the Romans left, the Moorish invaders brought new prosperity during their almost 400-year reign, calling it Hizn Quazri. Cáceres was finally

Francisco Pizarro in Trujillo

reconquered by King Alfonso IX of León in 1229 and repopulated by families from León, Asturias and Galicia who would later become the nobility of the region. The Order of Santiago, a brotherhood of knights, was founded here in the late 11th century, but it was not until the 16th century that the beautiful palaces and houses that give Cáceres its unique character were constructed.

From the **Plaza Mayor** you can pass through the **Arco de la Estrella** (Star Arch) into the **Old Town** and wander down a warren of streets lined with imposing buildings, sporting ostentatious heraldic shields and often topped by huge storks' nests. The **Casa de las Veletas** (Weathervane House) has been turned into a **provincial museum** featuring archaeological finds and displays of historical costumes and local customs, and has an old *ajibe* (Arabic reservoir) in the basement.

Trujillo

The hilltop skyline of **Trujillo** includes a heavily fortified **castillo**, which dominates the surrounding countryside, and the town is a worthy monument to its conquistador patrons. The eccentrically shaped **Plaza Mayor** has an interesting mix of buildings. On the southwestern corner stands the **Palacio del Marqués de la Conquista**, which was built by a renowned local soldier, Hernando Pizarro. An equestrian statue of his half-brother, Francisco, stands on the square.

There are half a dozen other palaces around the town, decorated with heroic portals, historic escutcheons and pretty patios – all worthy of investigation. Storks' nests crown the clock tower over the Gothic church of **San Martin**, which has a long, dark nave paved with ancient tombstones. The Romanesque and Gothic church of **Santa María la Mayor** boasts a fine *retablo* in Hispano-Flemish style. Two imposing stone seats on the balcony were built for the Catholic Monarchs, Fernando and Isabel.

Guadalupe

The turrets, spires and crenellations of the rambling **Monasterio de Nuestra Señora de Guadalupe** dominate the city from near and far. Surrounded by a huddle of small streets and squares the monastery – covering an area of about 2 hectares (5 acres) – is Spain's fourth most important pilgrimage site, and guardian of a precious wooden statue of the Virgin of Guadalupe, patron saint of the conquistadors. Founded in the 14th century, and enlarged four centuries

---

Sons of Trujillo

Of all the conquistador towns, none is more proud of its sons' exploits than Trujillo. The most famous were the Pizarros, who conquered Peru, but other natives were Diego García and Francisco de las Casas, who both founded towns called Trujillo in Venezuela and Honduras respectively, and Francis Orellana, the first European navigator of the Amazon.

Diego García in particular had a fearsome reputation. He was known as the Extremadura Samson and among his legendary feats of strength he is said to have picked up the font in Santa María la Mayor to carry holy water to his mother. The tombs of the Pizarros and that of García can be seen in the same church.

later, the monastery is an architectural hybrid, with a flamboyant façade flanked by stern defensive towers, and with Mudéjar and Gothic cloisters. Guided tours visit the cloisters, an embroidery museum, the chapter house, and the sacristy, which houses a remarkable collection of paintings by Zurbarán and others.

Badajoz

The gateway to Portugal, Badajoz is the biggest city in Extremadura. The medieval walled city is entered through the Puerta de Palmas – an ancient fortified city gate. Another arch used to bar the way to the **citadel** overlooking the Guadiana river, where the rulers of the Moorish kingdom of Badajoz held sway. The **cathedral**, founded in the 13th century, with its heavy walls and pinnacled tower, is largely Gothic but with Renaissance additions. Inside are impressive choir stalls, paintings, tapestries and tombstones. The **Museo Provincial de Bellas Artes**, which exhibits some good Flemish tapestries, is on the same square.

Mérida and Zafra

At the end of the Cantabrian Wars, Caesar Augustus chose to settle veteran legionnaires in the province of Lusitania. And in 25BC, Augusta Emerita was chosen to house veterans of

---

Alcántara – The Bridge

In its day, the magnificent six-arched Roman bridge over the Tagus near Alcántara was a renowned engineering feat. No less than 194m (636ft) long, with extraordinarily high arches, it is so impressive that the town was named after it: in Arabic al-Qantara means 'the bridge'. Built entirely without mortar, the bridge has stood since its completion in AD105.

the 5th and 10th legions. Not long after, it was designated as capital for the province and it soon grew to be the most important city in the Iberian Peninsula, and one of the most important in the Roman Empire. Today **Mérida**, a sleepy modern town and capital of Extremadura, can lay claim to the greatest number of Roman remains in any Spanish town.

Mérida's amphitheatre

The *pièce de résistance* is the partially restored 1st-century BC **Teatro Romano**, with seating for more than 5,500 spectators where, in summer, Greek and Roman plays are produced. The elliptical **Anfiteatro** next door (also known as the Circus Maximus) was designed to hold 15,000 spectators for gladiatorial contests and chariot races. At times it was even flooded in order to host recreations of great naval battles.

Almost next door is the **Museo Nacional de Arte Romano**. Its beautifully displayed collections include examples of Roman statuary, locally minted coins, and paintings discovered on the podium of the arena. Around town are many other Roman monuments: a temple to Diana, an aqueduct, and a 0.8-km (½-mile) bridge spanning the Guadiana.

Zafra is the most attractive of southern Extremadura's towns, and is often referred to as **Sevilla la Chica** (Little Sevilla). Its charming white houses converge on two arcaded plazas – Plaza Grande and Plaza Chica – recalling its Moorish origins. The medieval **Alcázar**, now a sumptuous *parador*, was where adventurer Hernán Cortés stayed before setting off to conquer Mexico.

Glorious Cala en Turqueta, in the southwest of Menorca

THE BALEARIC ISLANDS

In the western Mediterranean, the Balearics comprise a sunny cross-section of landscapes from mountainous Mallorca to the flat Formentera.

Mallorca

For decades **Mallorca** (Majorca as it is known by some in the English-speaking world) has been Europe's playground. The island measures 72km (45 miles) by 96km (60 miles), and well over half of the population lives in the animated and cosmopolitan capital city of **Palma de Mallorca**. **La Seu**, the formidable Gothic cathedral, was founded in 1299 – after the Reconquest by Jaume I (the Conqueror) – and dominates the seafront. The interior's magnificent proportions and traditional splendour are enhanced by Gaudí's *baldachin* hanging over the main altar.

Alongside is the island's most important building, the classical-style **Palau de l'Almudaina**, with delicately arched and covered balconies, which was once a palace for the Muslim governors. After the Reconquest, it was renovated for the medieval kings of Mallorca.

High on the hill overlooking Palma and commanding both the land and sea approaches, is the distinctive cylindrical silhouette of the tower of the 14th-century **Castell de Bellver**.

Exploring Mallorca's 965-km (600-mile) long coastline clockwise from Palma, the first stop must be the new marina and restaurant complex of **Portals Nous**, where the size of the yachts is sure to impress. High-rise **Magaluf**, though, is attractive mainly to the Brits who flock there in tens-of-thousands. **Port d'Andratx** lies close to the western tip of the island, on a sheltered bay popular with boating fans. **Banyalbufar**, to the north, has some of the island's finest terraced orchards, and **Esporlas** has the **La Granja**, a cross between a stately home, craft centre, traditional farmhouse and museum of rural life.

Valldemosa, which lies just inland, is a magnet for tourists who come to visit the monastery of **La Real Cartuja**, built on top of a royal castle. In it, you can see exhibits relating to the novelist George Sand and her companion, Frédéric Chopin, who rented rooms here between 1838 and 1839.

Turning back to the coast road, which in itself is a challenge, the next stop is **Deía**, probably the island's most attractive town, a pretty hilltop community built from honey-coloured stone.

Palma Cathedral

Attractive Deía

Something of an artists' colony – Robert Graves, the English poet and novelist, author of *I, Claudius*, is buried in the cemetery – this is also a good base for visiting the **Tramuntana** region in the northwest. A favourite haunt of the independent traveller, there are few beaches here, but a spectacular – and hair-raising – road allows fantastic views.

The town of **Sóller** is linked to Palma by a delightful narrow-gauge railway, with polished wood carriages making the hour-long journey through orchards and then mountain scenery. An old San Francisco-style open tram then travels the short journey down to the seaside and the pretty harbor of **Port de Sóller**.

The road between Sóller and Pollença is difficult and not particularly interesting, with the exception of the **Monastir de Lluc**, home to *La Moreneta* (the Black Madonna). **Pollença** itself is worth a visit to see the *Calvario* and a Roman bridge, while the nearby **Port de Pollença** is a very pleasant resort, not spoilt too much by tourism. To the north are the isolated and splendid cliffs of the **Cap de Formentor**. Continuing south, you will find the walled town of **Alcúdia** with its Roman ruins and popular Sunday market, and the busy beach resort of **Port d'Alcúdia**.

The main town at the easternmost end of the island is **Cala Ratjada**, a combined port and resort. **Porto Cristo**, further south, is a pleasant resort built around a protected harbour. One of the most popular tourist excursions on Mallorca, however, is a trip to the nearby **Coves del Drac** (Dragon's

Caves), where you can see dramatically lit formations, and the similar **Coves de Artà**.

There are several other small towns around the lower east and southern coastlines, but none of any consequence until you arrive at **El Arenal** and the other resorts that combine to make the **Bay of Palma** the busiest area on Mallorca.

Menorca

The second largest of the Balearic Islands, Menorca is one-fifth the area of Mallorca, and receives a much smaller number of visitors. It is a very pleasant, green and undulating island dotted with coastal towns and resorts as well as many scenic beaches and coves – some of which can only be reached on foot or by four-wheel-drive vehicle.

The capital and deep-water harbour of **Mahón** (Maó in Menorquí, the local language) was occupied by the British for a large part of the 18th century. The little city clusters on the cliffs above the port, and buildings in the older quarter of town have a distinctly Georgian appearance. A boat trip around the harbour makes a fun excursion.

Ciudadela (Ciutadella), on the west coast, also has a fine harbour, but is more akin to Andalucía than old England. **Ses Voltes**, the street leading to the Gothic cathedral that was begun in the 14th century, is all archways and completely

---

Menorca's Pre-history

Less visited than its beaches, but nonetheless well worth closer inspection, are the numerous megalithic structures that dot the Menorcan landscape. Known by their various types as *talayots*, *taules* and *navetas*, they were built between 2000 and 800BC. During this period a civilisation developed in the western Mediterranean that has become known on the Balearic Islands as the Talayot culture.

Ciutadella, Menorca

Moorish. Visit the city museum in the **Town Hall** (Ayuntamiento) for its rather curious exhibits on the history of the island.

The best beach and resort on the island is **Cala Santa Galdana**, a beautiful horseshoe-shaped cove developed in a restrained fashion. Further along the coast, on the way to Maó, is the **Cova d'en Xoroi**, and it shouldn't be missed. Here caves in the tall cliffs have been made into an innovative bar with fantastic views. **Fornells**, on the north coast, is another relaxed resort which also remains an active fishing port.

Ibiza (Eivissa)

Besides those simply seeking some sun and sea, Ibiza these days caters to the seriously hip, from assorted rock stars and artists to dance-crazy youths, and offers accommodation, restaurants, shops and entertainment accordingly.

Ibiza Town (Eivissa), the island's capital, is dominated by its old town, **Dalt Vila**, whose encircling walls are the longest in Spain. Within the walls you will find a cobbled maze packed with whitewashed houses, tiny bars, shops, flea markets and restaurants serving local fare. The capital has two archaeological museums containing a treasury of Carthaginian art. One, the **Puig des Molins**, is built adjacent to a necropolis, and tours of the burial chambers are given.

It is the beaches, though, that most people come for. They start immediately south of town, but the best, and certainly the trendiest, are generally agreed to be those at **Las Salinas**. **Santa Eularia**, to the north, is an important resort, as is **Sant Antoni** on the west coast, though this is very much the land of the cheap package holiday. **Portinatx** and **San Miguel**, in the north, are much smaller and quieter resorts, and you can visit caves at San Miguel.

The bright lights, loud music, exotic dress codes and, it must be said, the easy availability of drugs attract young people from all over northern Europe to Ibiza. The clubs to which they are attracted are found, mainly, in the south of the island. Typical of these is **Privilege** which, at 7,000 sq m (1.73 acres) has a capacity of 10,000 people, and advertises itself as the largest dance club in the world.

Enjoying Ibiza's nightlife

Formentera

The 11-km (7-mile) sea voyage from Ibiza takes 75 minutes by boat, or around half that by hydrofoil, but, whichever you choose, it's more often than not a rough passage. There is no airport here, and very little water, which has hindered large-scale development.

Once the sole retreat of the backpacker and laid-back beach bum, Formentera now caters for package tourists who come for the extensive, unspoiled beaches. There is not much to do here besides sunbathing and windsurfing.

THE CANARY ISLANDS

The seven inhabited volcanic islands that form the Canaries in the Atlantic, just off the coast of North Africa, are as different from each other as can possibly be and provide a semi-tropical escape for those in search of winter sun.

The Canaries are split into two provinces: Santa Cruz de Tenerife consists of the westernmost islands of Tenerife, little-visited El Hierro, La Gomera and La Palma; the eastern province of Las Palmas de Gran Canaria has Gran Canaria, Lanzarote and Fuerteventura. The islands appeal to differing tastes – some are better for walking, others for beach holidays.

Tenerife

The largest of the Canaries, Tenerife offers more attractions and more contrasts than any of its island neighbours. **Santa Cruz de Tenerife**, in the northeast, is the administrative capital of the westerly Canaries. Most tourists head for the baking beaches of **Los Cristianos** and **Playa Los Américas** in the south. The island's first resort, however, was **Puerto de la Cruz** on the attractive north coast, despite having no beach. This deficiency has been overcome by the genius of the late César Manrique who designed **Lago Martiánez**, a 3-hectare (8-acre) complex of tropical lagoons, cascading fountains and sunbathing terraces cleverly landscaped with lush palms and volcanic rocks to blend perfectly into the seafront. Nearby **Loro**

Before the arrival of Europeans, the Canary Islands were inhabited by a people known as the Guanches, or 'sons of the earth'. Much has been discovered about their culture, including the fact that they mummified their dead and buried them in caves. Scientists place their ethnic origins in northwest Africa.

Puerto de la Cruz, Tenerife

Parque is a delight for all ages. It has the world's largest collection of parrots – more than 300 species and subspecies. It is also home to an eclectic array of animals, including gorillas, chimpanzees, tigers, jaguars, alligators, sea-lions, dolphins and numerous other creatures that are exhibited in carefully and creatively designed spaces.

Jardín Botánico, founded by royal decree in 1788, is the oldest local attraction. It lies on the road to **Orotava**, the island's most picturesque town, with colonial homes and immense, traditional balconies. **La Laguna**, a World Heritage Site, preserves the impressive architecture of the early Spanish conquerors. On the north side of the island is the intriguing **Pirámides de Güímar**, where the late explorer and resident Thor Heyerdahl set out his theories about how Europeans reached the New World long ago.

The highlight of the island in every sense, **Mt Teide** is a volcanic cone in the **Las Cañadas del Teide National Park**,

Teide, Spain's highest mountain

and is Spain's highest mountain at 3,717m (12,200ft). Particularly beautiful in May and June when the wildflowers are in bloom, the park's spectacular scenery makes for great hiking. It is strange in mid-winter to see this gigantic snow-capped peak dominating beaches full of sun bathers and swimmers. The visitor centre has details of walking trails and guided walks. You can also get to within 163m (535ft) of the summit by cable car *(teleférico)*, though you need to arrive early to avoid queues.

La Gomera

La Gomera remains an unspoiled island of steep, green terraced hills and tranquil valleys. Boats and hydrofoils make the short trip from Los Cristianos, arriving at **San Sebastián**. The main town, it is notable for its connections with Christopher Columbus, including a local church where he prayed and the house where he supposedly stayed in 1492. A delight for walkers, the **Garajonay National Park** is a World Heritage Site and home to the **Alto de Garajonay**, Gomera's highest peak – 1,487m (4,878ft). The island's only beach resort is in the south, at the low-key **Playa de Santiago**.

La Palma

The most northwesterly of the Canaries, La Palma is lush and green. **Santa Cruz de la Palma**, the capital, is an appealing small town. The main attraction here is the magnificent **Caldera de Taburiente**, a giant crater that has a circumference of some 27km (17 miles) and which drops around 700m (2,300ft) into a fertile valley. The island is perfect walking country, with marvellous views. The world-renowned Palma **observatory**, open to the public only for a few days each summer, is on top of the **Roque de los Muchachos**, the highest peak in Palma at 2,423m (7,950ft).

Gran Canaria

Almost circular in shape, Gran Canaria has been described as a continent in miniature. The coastline ranges from awesome cliffs to golden dunes; inland, you can choose between stark mountains and tranquil valleys. It is also well supplied with beaches, shopping centres and sophisticated nightlife.

Typical Canarian balconies

    Las Palmas, capital of the island, is a major commercial centre, cosmopolitan resort and port. Its old town, **Vegueta**, with the handsome governor's residence, the 15th-century **Casa de Colón**, has well-preserved colonial architecture. The **Playa de las Canteras**, the town's sandy, restaurant-lined beach, is 3km (2 miles) long and the **Parque Santa Catalina** is one big outdoor café that buzzes night and day.

On the promenade, Maspalomas

The main beach resorts are on the island's south coast. Maspalomas, or Costa Canaria, is a mega-resort made up of three parts. **Playa del Inglés** is a large, crowded package-tour centre. **Maspalomas** proper is famous for its Sahara-like dunes, which are known as an unofficial nudist beach, while **San Agustín** is quiet and tidy. West of Maspalomas, **Puerto Rico** is a family-oriented resort and **Puerto de Mogán** is an attractive fishing 'village'. **Cruz de Tejeda**, at 1,463m (4,800ft), is a popular vantage point in the rugged centre of the island, and the panorama includes two distinctive rock formations once worshipped by the Guanches *(see page 124)*.

Lanzarote

Lanzarote is a startling place, representing the triumph of civilisation over a hostile environment. Declared a Biosphere Reserve by UNESCO, the island is pock-marked with over 300 volcanoes. The locals grow onions, tomatoes, potatoes, melons and grapes, which spring in abundance from the volcanic ash. Lanzarote was the birthplace of César Manrique whose eclectic sculptures and architectural creations enhance the island. His creativity can be seen at the **Fundación César Manrique** art gallery, the prickly Jardín de Cactus, the caves of Jameos del Agua, the Monumento al Campesino and the Mirador del Río, which offers spectacular views.

Arrecife is the undistinguished capital. The island's main resort, **Puerto del Carmen**, lies to the south and has a long, golden beach, while **Costa Teguise**, just to the north of

Arrecife, offers more upmarket facilities. The highlight of a trip to Lanzarote is a visit to the **Montañas de Fuego** ('Mountains of Fire') in the **Timanfaya National Park**. The stark but scenically magnificent park starts just north of **Yaiza**. Its bizarre landscape of lava flows and rust-red mountains was formed over 16 months of cataclysmic volcanic activity during 1730–1. There is an information centre and car park at **Islote de Hilario**, from where bus tours depart to explore the incredible lunar landscape.

Fuerteventura

Situated less than 100km (60 miles) off the coast of North Africa, and just south of Lanzarote, Fuerteventura is a bather's paradise. There are miles of golden sandy beaches, and the winds that originally blew the sand here from the Sahara still ensure superb windsurfing, for which the **Playa de Sotavento** is famous. At the southern tip of the island, the **Jandía** peninsula offers great beaches, the best of which are on the less-developed **Costa Calma**. Besides watersports there is little else to do on this treeless island. **Betancuria**, the first capital, is an isolated inland oasis, and its splendid 17th-century church of **Santa Maria** is worth a visit.

Betancuria on Fuerteventura

WHAT TO DO

A s well as its historical attractions, Spain is blessed with marvellous beaches and an incredibly varied coastline. Some of Spain's resorts are very popular and crowded in the main season, but even the famous Costa del Sol still has relatively wild and undeveloped areas, and those seeking quieter resorts do not have to look very far to find them.

WATERSPORTS

Fishing. For freshwater fishing, including fly fishing, especially in the Pyrenees and Cantabria, approach local tourist offices for permits. There is game fishing in the Canary Islands.

Scuba diving. There is good diving off the Costa Brava around the protected Medes islands, on the Costa de Almería, Costa Tropical and the Balearic Islands. The Canary Islands offer greater variety in deep Atlantic dives. Operators can arrange tuition, permits and equipment hire.

Water-skiing. Large resorts are fully equipped for water-skiing, jet-skiing and parasailing. The calmer waters of the Balearics and east-coast resorts at La Manga, Costa Dorada and Costa Brava are all good places to try these sports.

Windsurfing. Tuition, equipment and wetsuit hire are available almost everywhere. Advanced windsurfers chase the high winds of Tarifa in southern Spain *(see page 82)* or pick up the steady trade winds on the Jandía peninsula, Fuerteventura, and Medina, Tenerife, in the Canary Islands.

LAND SPORTS

Golf. Spain is famous for golf, with more than 100 courses on the mainland and islands. Not every pro is a Sevvy

Sun, sea and sand in Ibiza

Ballesteros, but the quality of instruction is generally high. The greatest concentration of courses is on the Costa del Sol, where road signs declare this also to be the Costa del Golf. On the east coast, the Valencian courses of El Saler and Escorpión are highly rated and of good value; La Manga Club on the Costa Cálida has three championship courses. On the islands, Mallorca has a number of fine courses, while Gran Canaria has Spain's oldest golf club, in a stunning setting. For an overview of what's available, request a golfing map of Spain from the national tourist office.

Tennis. Many hotels and villa complexes have their own tennis courts – some even have a resident professional. The Costa del Sol is probably the biggest centre for tennis tuition and on the east coast La Manga Club is one of the best tennis centres in Europe.

Horseriding. There are ranches and equestrian centres all over the country. Many offer instruction and a range of outings on horseback, from a stimulating cross-country excursion to an overnight trek. A favourite place for this sport is

---

Jai-Alai – The World's Fastest Ball Game

The ancient Basque game of jai-alai (pronounced 'high-a-lie', but sometimes also known as *pelota*) is played throughout the Basque region. Every town and almost every village, no matter how tiny, has a *frontón*, or pitch, rather like a squash court, where the players hurl themselves around after the *pelota* (ball), which is propelled at the back wall at speeds of up to 300km/h (188mph) by woven straw scoops attached to the players' hands.

The basic rules are similar to those for tennis or squash – the ball may only bounce once on the ground; each game comprises 7 to 9 points. Considerably more complex is the betting, which is largely incomprehensible to outsiders.

the Alpujarra region, south of the Sierra Nevada.

Skiing. Most skiing resorts are in the Pyrenees range (including Andorra) and the Picos de Europa. In the south of the country, the Sierra Nevada resort of Solynieve, just outside Granada, is also well known,

Walking, hiking and climbing. Spain has a well-marked network of long-distance

Cycling in Galicia

footpaths denominated 'GR'. National, regional and local tourist offices can supply further information. Nature reserves and scenic areas have shorter hiking trails graded according to the difficulty of the terrain, from *baja* (easy) to *muy alta* (for experienced walkers only).

SHOPPING

Shops in Spain are as well equipped as elsewhere in Europe, but fans of the truly kitsch should have no fear, for among the genuinely tasteful souvenirs of a Spanish holiday – ceramics, leather goods, food treats from olive oil to nougat – the straw donkey and bullfight poster are still alive and well.

For a quick survey of what Spaniards are buying, browse through the big department stores, such as the ubiquitous El Corte Inglés. There are branches in major cities, and unlike the majority of Spanish businesses they stay open through the lunch-and-siesta break and until about 9pm.

For quality crafts, it's best to seek out the workshops of local artisans. Tourist offices will always be able to advise on their locations.

Fans for keeping cool

Here are a few suggestions for best buys in Spain:

Antiques. You will find few bargains in genuine antiques shops or stalls. However, some big cities have open-air *rastros* (flea markets) on Sunday mornings – those in Madrid and Sevilla are attractions in their own right – which can provide plenty of fun for browsers.

Artificial pearls. Made in Mallorca, these are so convincing that experts are often fooled. Some say the test is to rub them along your teeth – the real ones are more gritty.

Ceramics. Each region has its own distinctive designs and colour schemes. Hand-painted *azulejos* (tiles of Moorish origins) are popular and collectable. Talavera de la Reina, west of Madrid, is a major centre for top-rated ceramics. Lladró figurine collectors can stock up at stores all over Spain; less detailed models from the same workshop (based in Valencia) go under the name of Nao porcelain.

Damascene and Toledo steel. This is a speciality of Toledo, although the art of damascening (inlaying the steel with intricate gold designs) originated in Damascus.

Embroidery and lace. Pretty embroidered linen and traditional lacework is sold all over Spain. Look for lace *mantillas*, those lightweight shawls used for covering the shoulders, often worn over a comb in the hair. Be wary of street sellers offering bargain prices; their goods are generally of much poorer quality and made anywhere but in Spain.

Glassware. Mallorca is a centre for glassmaking. The typical blue, green or amber bowls, glasses and jugs are sold in many mainland stores.

Leather. Top-quality Spanish leather products range from sturdy belts, wallets and riding boots to elegant handbags and jackets. Beware of the less expensive bags and belts on sale at stalls and in markets; more often than not these are imported from Morocco and you will pay two to three times the original price.

ENTERTAINMENT

Since Spaniards don't start thinking about their dinner until 9 or 10pm, Spanish nightlife tends to keep going far later than in other countries. After a leisurely meal, it's on to the music bar (occasionally live music, but generally a video screen pumping up the volume) for a drink and a chance to catch the latest football score before deciding where to go next. Only then will they actually hit the disco or nightclub – around 2am. Barcelona is one of the most fashionable nightspots in Europe. Madrid is the city that never sleeps, and Ibiza is the leader of Europe's clubbing scene.

Flamenco

Throbbing guitars, snapping fingers, stamping heels, colourful dresses and soul-stirring songs lure local enthusiasts and visitors to Spain's flamenco nightclubs. There are two main groups of songs: the bouncier, more cheerful type is known as *cante chico*; the *cante jonto* deals with love, death and human drama in slow, piercing style. Unfortunately, most people will only get to see the show-biz style *tablaos* flamenco, for which their hotel gets a percentage for every ticket sold. For the real thing, you have to head

Bullfighting

Like it or loathe it, it is impossible to escape the impact that the *corrida* (bullfight) has on Spanish life. The colourful *carteles* (advertising posters) are ubiquitous in Spain and the *temporada* (season) lasts from March to October. The bullfight isn't considered a sport – a contest between two equals. Instead it is a highly ritualistic event in which man pits himself against a magnificent and powerful animal.

The *corrida* consists of three *tercios* (acts), each with its own rituals. In the first *tercio*, the *toro bravo* (fighting bull) is released and the matador (literally 'killer') takes stock of the bull, making passes with his large magenta and yellow *capote* (cape). Next the *picadores* – mounted men armed with wooden poles tipped with a *puya*, a pointed metal head – attempt to lance the bull behind its *morillo* (large neck muscle), causing the bull's head to lower.

In the second *tercio*, the *banderilleros*, part of the matador's *cuadrilla* (team of assistants) work on foot to plant long sticks with a barbed end and covered with coloured paper into the bull's back.

The third and final *tercio*, the *faena*, sees the matador return, without his *montera* (hat) and armed with just the much smaller, dark red *muleta* (cape). This is what he gets paid handsomely for. For the next 13 minutes – legally it cannot last any longer, and often it is shorter – he adjusts his skills to the characteristics and strength of the bull, with intricate passes that bring man and bull into close harmony. If all is going well, the band will strike up an accompanying *pasodoble*; but when the matador is ready for the 'moment of truth', the most dangerous point in the *corrida*, the band will unceremoniously stop.

It is then that the matador, *muleta* in his left hand directing the bull's attention away from his body and sword in his right, will spin over the dangerous right horn, trying to deliver an *espada* (sword) stroke between the shoulder blades and into the heart, with the aim of killing the bull instantly.

for the specialist bars and clubs of Andalucía, home of flamenco, and it's best to ask a taxi driver to take you to them as the performers often move from one to another without much notice. In Madrid, Casa Patas in La Latina district is a good introduction to flamenco.

Other Cultural Activities

Spaniards take opera very seriously, along with their home-grown stars Plácido Domingo, José Carreras, Teresa Berganza and Monserrat Caballé. There are three great venues: Barcelona's Gran Teatre del Liceu, Madrid's Teatro Real and Sevilla's Teatro de la Maestranza.

For concerts, Madrid's Auditorio Nacional de Música, inaugurated in 1988, is home to the Spanish National Orchestra. Check with local tourist offices for details of concerts and recitals in other cities. They often take place in historic surroundings, especially in summer.

For drama, Spanish as well as foreign plays – classical and contemporary – can be seen all over the country.

Foreign films are generally dubbed before they are shown in a Spanish cinema, but in major cities and some resorts cinemas may show films in their original version (labelled 'v.o.') with Spanish subtitles.

CHILDREN

Long, sunny days and soft, safe, sandy beaches mean that coastal Spain is a favourite family destination. Many hotels have special features for junior guests,

Flamenco is music to stir the depths of the soul

ranging from organised poolside games and outings to babysitting facilities. When seawater and sandcastles start to wear thin, you can try some of the following:

Make a splash. Water parks are a highly popular alternative. While some choose to shoot down waterslides and ride the machine-made waves, the less active types can top off their tans in landscaped gardens. Additional attractions often include ten-pin bowling and mini-golf.

Go-karting. A favourite with the children (not to mention their parents), go-kart tracks are common along the *costas* and in the islands.

A night out. The Spanish take their children out at night, so why not do likewise? Older children will probably enjoy a colourful flamenco show, and there are no restrictions on children accompanying adults into bars, restaurants or cafés, as long as they are well behaved.

Fiesta. Older children will love the firework displays and music, while the younger ones watch the dancers and giant papier-mâché figures wide-eyed. Carnival is always a colourful event, where the local children usually wear the best costumes. There is nothing to stop you from also dressing up and joining in. It's enormous fun and you're sure to be made welcome.

The fun of the fair. Most big towns or resorts have a *parque de atracciones* where the rides range from the old-fashioned carousel and big wheel to high-tech thrills. Barcelona's funfair at Tibidabo, accessible by funicular railway, deserves a special mention for its old-fashioned rides and tremendous views over the city and countryside.

Theme parks. Spain's biggest theme parks are Port Aventura on the Costa Dorada, Terra Mitica near Benidorm, Isla Magica in Seville, Warner Brothers Movie World outside Madrid, Palmitos Park on Gran Canaria and Loro Parque on Tenerife.

Festivals

The best way to experience Spanish customs is to experience a *fiesta* (festival), held in honour of the local patron saint and offering locals the chance to dress up in costume, dance through the night, let of firecrackers or run with bulls. Every community, whatever its size, has its own *fiesta* – with the larger towns and cities often celebrating more than one. Check with the tourist office for details of local celebrations during your stay. Here's a selection of the very best from around the country:

February/March: Carnival before the beginning of Lent. Processions in Santa Cruz de Tenerife, Cádiz, Sitges and many other places.

March/April: Las Falllas Festival in Valencia, with the setting alight of hundreds of papier-mâché figures. Semana Santa (Holy Week). Processions of hooded penitents in all major cities from Palm Sunday until Easter Sunday, with the most famous in Sevilla.

April: Sevilla's famous Feria (Spring Fair) with colourful costume parades, plenty of *sevillana* music, and bullfights.

May: Festival of the Patios in Córdoba and International Horse Fair in Jerez de la Frontera.

May/June: Fiesta de San Isidro: bullfighting, concerts and funfairs in Madrid. Corpus Christi: festivities in Granada, Toledo, Sitges and the Canary Islands.

July: Fiesta de San Fermín: bullruns, bullfights and festivities in Pamplona. Festival of the Virgen del Carmen, patroness of fishermen. Festival of St James, Santiago de Compostela, with firework displays and bonfires.

August: Assumption: national holiday on August 15 with numerous towns holding festivals.

September: Logroño Wine Harvest: wine festival in Jerez de la Frontera. Mercé Feria de San Miguel, Torremolinos. Meced Festival: music and folklore in Barcelona.

October: Pilar Festival: processions, bullfights and folklore in Zaragoza.

December: Fiesta de Verdiales: flamenco festival in Málaga.

EATING OUT

The Spanish take their food very seriously and you will rarely be disappointed by the variety and flavour of the hearty portions served in local *restaurantes* throughout Spain. Each region has its own distinctive culinary strengths, from the seafood creations of the north to the rice platters of the east, from the roasts of the central area to the succulent hams and fried fish of the south. And for every dish, there is usually a locally grown wine to match.

Tucking into some fish at a coastal resort

WHERE TO EAT

Venta, posada, mesón, casa de comidas and *fonda* are all synonyms for 'restaurant'. Many bars also double as restaurants, serving both tapas and full meals. The menu will be displayed outside or at the door, giving an idea of what you can expect to pay. *(See Recommended Restaurants page 182.)*

Most restaurants offer a good value *menú del día* (daily special). This is normally a three-course meal, including house wine, at a reasonable set price, although it may only be available at lunchtime.

The prices on the menu include a service charge and

taxes, but it is customary to leave a tip of 5 to 10 percent if you have been served efficiently. Bars and cafés, like restaurants, usually include a service charge, but additional small tips of a few coins are customary. Prices are slightly lower if you stand or sit at the bar rather than occupy a table.

Two notes of caution: the prices of *tapas*, those tasty bar snacks, are not always indicated and can be surprisingly expensive: it is not unusual for the cost of several *tapas* to equate to or exceed the price of the *menú del día*. Also, ask how much your meal will cost when ordering fish or seafood that is priced by the 100g weight. The price is based on the uncooked weight and can be more than you expected.

Meal times are generally later in Spain than in most parts of Europe. Temperatures dictate how the day is structured and what is the best time to eat. Peak hours are 2–3.30pm for lunch and 9–11pm for dinner. In Madrid and the south, meals are eaten very late, starting at around 10pm. However, in tourist areas or big cities, you can get a meal at most places just about any time of day.

WHAT TO EAT

Breakfast

For Spaniards, this is the least significant meal of the day and will probably just consist of *tostada* (toast) or a roll and coffee. If you have a sweet tooth, *churros* are deep-fried sugared doughnut-like temptations, made for dipping into your coffee. To make guests feel at home, most hotels offer breakfast buffets with a selection of cereals, fresh and dried fruit, cold meats and cheeses, plus bacon and eggs.

Lunch and Dinner

The classic Spanish dish is *paella*, named after the black iron pan in which saffron-flavoured rice is cooked in stock. True

Valencian *paella* is made with chicken and rabbit, but there is also a seafood variety and many restaurants serve a 'mixed' variety, which can have all sorts of ingredients. It is always cooked to order (usually for a minimum of two people) and outside of tourist areas is normally served only at lunch.

There are two other national favourites well known to visitors. The first is *gazpacho*, a delicious Andalucían chilled soup made with chopped tomatoes, peppers, cucumbers, onions and fried croutons. The second is *tortilla*, or potato omelette. There are many variations on this theme, served hot or cold.

Regional Tastes

Every province – and almost every town – in Spain seems to have its own locally produced sausage, cheese or variation on *cocido*, a rich cold-weather meat and vegetable hot-pot. Here are a few suggestions for what's cooking around the country, moving roughly north to south.

Tapas

A *tapa* is a small portion of food, usually served with a slice or two of French bread, which encourages you to keep drinking instead of heading off to a restaurant for a meal. Once upon a time, *tapas* were given away, but that is rare these days. Even so, bars that specialise in *tapas* are more popular than ever.

Good *tapas* bars have a whole counter displaying hot and cold dishes, making it easy to make a choice – just point to one you like the look of. Typical offerings are olives, meatballs, local cheese, prawns in garlic, marinated anchovies, *chorizo* (spicy sausage), and wedges of Spanish *tortilla* (omelette). *Una tapa* is the smallest amount you can order; *una ración* is half a small plateful; and *una porción* is almost a meal in itself.

Galicia: Famed for great seafood, particularly *pulpo* (octopus); try also *caldo gallego* (a hearty vegetable soup), *empanada* (flaky pastry pies stuffed with meat or seafood, served hot or cold), *lacón con grelos* (boiled ham with turnip greens) and paprika-laced dishes.

Asturias: Look out for *fabada asturiana* (big white bean and sausage casserole), *merluza a la sidra* (hake in cider sauce), and *queso de Cabrales* (pungent, piquant, creamy blue cheese).

Cured hams are a speciality of the mountainous regions

Basque country: Seafood is king here, in the form of *bacalao al pil pil* (fried cod in hot garlic sauce), *chipirones* (tiny squid), *marmitako* (spicy tuna, tomato and potato stew) and *merluza con almejas y gambas* (hake with clams and prawns).

The Pyrenees: Hearty, warming meat dishes are served in *chilindrón* sauce (tomatoes, peppers, garlic, ham and wine); look out for game dishes, and mountain trout.

Catalonia: This region is noted for *esqueixada* salad (grilled or baked vegetables in olive oil), grilled fish with *romesco* sauce (nuts, chilli, tomatoes, garlic and breadcrumbs), and seafood stews, such as *zarzuela* and *suquet de peix*.

Castile: Try *sopa castellana* for starters (a baked garlic soup with chunks of ham and an egg poaching in it), followed by *cochinillo asado* (suckling pig) or *cordero asado* (roast lamb).

The east coast: Valencia is the original home of *paella* and many other rice-based dishes.

La Mancha: Quixote country is famed for such game dishes as *tojunto* (rabbit stew), but also for *pisto manchego*

Paella – the classic Spanish dish

(an extravagant ratatouille-like vegetable stew of red peppers, onions, aubergines, tomatoes and courgettes) and *manchego*, which is Spain's favourite cheese made with sheep's milk.

Extremadura: The region is noted for country-style pork and lamb and countless varieties of sausage.

Andalucía: Specialities in this region include cold soups, *gazpacho* and *ajo blanco* (or *gazpacho blanco*, made from garlic and almonds garnished with grapes), *fritura mixta* or *pescaito frito* (pieces of fish fried in a light batter) and *huevos a la flamenca* (egg, tomato and vegetable baked with *chorizo*, prawns and ham).

The Islands: Canarian specialities include *papas arrugadas* (new potatoes baked and rolled in rock salt) served with *mojo picón* (piquant red sauce) and *mojo verde* (green herb sauce served with fish). On Mallorca, sample *tumbet* (ratatouille and potato casserole with meat or fish).

Sweet-Tooth Specials

The ubiquitous Spanish dessert is the egg-based flan *(crème caramel)*. The Catalans do a deluxe version, *crema catalana*, which is flavoured with lemon and cinnamon, and many towns have their own recipes for *yemas*, a monumentally sweet egg-yolk and sugar confection.

Otherwise, you can head for the *pastelerías* (cake shops) for a vast repertoire of cakes, tarts and pastries. *Mazapan* (marzipan) and *turrón* (nougat) also come in various guises, with regional variations.

WHAT TO DRINK

Wines and Alcoholic Drinks

Spain has more square kilometres of vineyards than any other European country. Vintage pundits confidently compare the best Spanish wines with the most respected French classics, causing much controversy in some global wine circles. On the other hand, much of the crop is ordinary, intended for home consumption and never meant to grace the glasses of experts or travel far.

The better Spanish wines are regulated by the Denominación de Origen quality control. If a bottle is marked DOC, you can be sure the wine was made in a particular region and its producers followed the strictest rules.

Sampling wine in a bodega

The oldest and most vigorously protected wine *denominación* is Rioja, and some truly distinguished reds (*tinto*) are grown along the Ebro Valley in northern Spain. East of La Rioja, Aragon contributes some powerful Cariñena reds and Ribera del Duero also produces quality reds. The best-known wines from central Spain, the splendidly smooth reds of Valdepeñas, come from La Mancha.

The Penedés region of Catalonia is acclaimed not only for its excellent still white wines *(blanco)*, but also for its *cava*, a sparkling wine made by the *methode champenoise*; it is a revitalising and refreshing chilled drink.

In the southwest, Jerez de la Frontera is the home of sherry. As an aperitif, try a chilled, dry *fino* or medium-dry *amontillado*. A dark, sweet *oloroso* goes down well after dinner. Spain also produces several sweet dessert wines, such as muscatel, which tastes of sultanas and honey.

Spanish brandy is often sweeter and heavier than French Cognac. It is a vital ingredient in *sangría* – a popular tourist drink – whose other ingredients are red wine, orange and lemon juice, mineral water, sugar, sliced fruit and ice.

Beer *(cerveza)* is generally of the pils, or lager, variety, and not very strong. There are plenty of Spanish brands, and foreign beers are widely available. A small draught beer is *una caña pequeña*, a medium size one is a *tubo* and a large one (not always available) – a *grande* – is about the same size as a pint. Bottled beer is sold in a one-third litre bottle – *una botella* – or a one-quarter litre bottle – *una botellin*. Bottles are more expensive than draught.

Tea, Coffee and Soft Drinks

The Spanish usually drink coffee *(café)* as opposed to tea *(té)*. This can be either *solo*, small and black; *con leche*, a large cup made with milk; or *cortado*, a small cup with a little milk. Americans may find Spanish coffee strong. Decaffeinated coffee *(descafeinado)* is served in the more cosmopolitan areas.

Mineral water *(agua mineral)* is either sparkling *(con gas)* or still *(sin gas)*. Ice cream parlours *(heladería)* sell *granizado*, slushy iced fruit juices, and many bars serve fresh orange juice *(zumo de naranjas naturales)*, though this can be surprisingly expensive considering oranges are one of Spain's main crops.

To Help You Order...

Could we have a table?   **¿Nos puede dar una mesa?**
Do you have a set menu? **¿Tiene un menú del día?**
I'd like...   **Quisiera...**

beer	**una cerveza**	milk	**leche**
bread	**pan**	mineral water	**agua mineral**
coffee	**un café**	potatoes	**patatas**
dessert	**un postre**	rice	**arroz**
fish	**pescado**	salad	**una ensalada**
fruit	**fruta**	sandwich	**un bocadillo**
glass	**un vaso**	sugar	**azúcar**
ice cream	**un helado**	tea	**un té**
meat	**carne**	water (iced)	**agua (fresca)**
menu	**la carta**	wine	**vino**

...and Read the Menu

aceitunas	olives	**langosta**	spiny lobster
albóndigas	meatballs	**langostino**	large prawn
almejas	baby clams	**lomo**	loin
atún	tuna	**mariscos**	shellfish
anchoas	anchovies	**mejillones**	mussels
bacalao	cod	**melocotón**	peach
besugo	sea bream	**merluza**	hake
boquerones	fresh anchovies	**navajas**	razor clams
calamares	squid	**ostras**	oysters
callos	tripe	**pastel**	cake
caracoles	snails	**pollo**	chicken
cerdo	pork	**pulpitos**	baby octopus
chuleta	chops	**salsa**	sauce
cocido	stew	**sepia**	squid
cordero	lamb	**ternera**	veal
entremeses	hors-d'oeuvre	**tortilla**	omelette
gambas	prawns	**trucha**	trout
habas	broad beans	**uvas**	grapes

HANDY TRAVEL TIPS

An A–Z Summary of Practical Information

A

ACCOMMODATION *(hotel; alojamiento*; see also CAMPING, YOUTH HOSTELS and the list of RECOMMENDED HOTELS).

Those travelling independently will find a wide range of options. For a comprehensive listing of accommodation and rates throughout Spain, consult the *Guía Oficial de Hoteles*, available from The Spanish National Tourist Office *(see Tourist Information Offices on page 170)* and some local bookshops.

By law, prices must be displayed in the reception and in the room showing seasonal adjustments. Meals (including breakfast) are not usually included in the basic price, and VAT (IVA in Spanish) will be added to your bill.

Establishments in Spain are graded by each of the 17 autonomous governments, and may vary from region to region. More expensive hotels will have air conditioning where necessary, and rooms will have showers. Hotels are rated according to the system detailed below, with one of the following ratings plus the appropriate number of stars:

Hotel (H): rated one to five stars according to services offered.

Hotel Residencia (HR): a hotel without a restaurant, but often with a bar and cafeteria facilities.

Motel (M): rated same as hotels; these are few and far between.

Hotel Apartamentos (HA): apartments with hotel services and facilities, and rated the same as hotels.

Residencia Apartamentos (RA): residential apartments without a restaurant, rated the same as hotels.

Hostal (Hs): a more modest hotel, often a family concern, graded one to three stars. Rates overlap with the lower range of hotels. A three-star *hostal* can cost about the same as a one or two-star hotel.

Hostal Residencia (HsR): a *hostal* without a restaurant.

Pensión (P): a boarding house, graded one to three stars, with only basic amenities and usually shared bathrooms.

Casa de Huéspedes (CH): a guesthouse. Bottom of the scale with simple facilities, but often clean and comfortable as well as cheap.

Ciudad de Vacaciones (CV): a hotel complex complete with sports facilities.

Casa Rural: a country or village house offering bed-and-breakfast or self-catering accommodation.

Parador: a state-run hotel, often housed in a castle or other historic building, always in a fine setting and furnished in local style. Prices are mostly in line with those of a four- to five-star hotel. Advance booking is advisable. For information and bookings in Spain contact the Paradores de Turismo, Central de Reservas, Requena, 3, 28013 Madrid, tel: 915 166 666, fax: 915 166 657 or <www.parador.es>; in the UK contact Keytel International, 402 Edgware Road, London W2 1ED, tel: (020) 7616 0300, fax: (020) 7616 0317; in the USA and Canada contact Marketing Ahead, 381 Park Avenue South, Suite 718, New York, NY, tel: 1 800 223-1356 or (212) 686-9213, fax: (212) 686-0271, e-mail <mahrep@aol.com>.

I'd like a single/double room with bath/shower.	**Quisiera una habitación sencilla/doble con baño/ducha.**
What's the rate per night?	**¿Cuál es el precio por noche?**

AIRPORTS *(aeropuertos*; see also GETTING THERE)

Madrid's Barajas Airport (14 km/9 miles northeast of the capital) is the main gateway to Spain from North America, but there are direct flights to Barcelona and Málaga. Other important international airports are Alicante, Almería, Jerez de la Frontera, Santiago de Compostela, Sevilla and Valencia. There are also major airports on Mallorca, Tenerife and Gran Canaria.

Madrid is Spain's main air transport hub, and airlines such as Iberia and Spanair offer frequent connections to regional airports throughout the country and to the Canary Islands and the Balearics.

B

BUDGETING FOR YOUR TRIP

Accommodation. Although Spain is still widely thought of as a budget destination, hotel prices in the cities can be comparable with other European cities. So if you are planning a city-based stay on a limited budget choose your accommodation carefully. Reasonably priced rooms are still widely available all over Spain. Rates for a double room can range from as low as €30–€40 at a *pensión* or *hostal* to as much as €360–€420, or even more, at a top-of-the-range 5-star hotel. As a rule of thumb, a good 4-star hotel will cost in the range of €100–€150. Prices normally exclude breakfast and IVA (value added tax).

Car hire. Car hire costs are generally lower than average for Europe, but prices vary, so shop around. Fly-drive deals are often good value. If you want a small, manual-transmission car primarily for local use, it is generally cheaper to hire from a local company, especially on the Costas and the islands. *(See also Car Hire on page 152.)*

Meals and drinks. While simple meals and drinks are good value, prices vary considerably, according to where you choose to eat. The cheapest three-course meal with one drink, *menú del día*, in a small bar/restaurant will be around €8–€10. Dinner in a medium-level restaurant will be about €18 per head, including wine. At the top restaurants expect to pay €40–€50 per person, or more, plus wine.

Entertainment. Approximate prices are: cinema from €4, flamenco nightclub (entry and first drink) from €18, discotheque from €6, amusement park (per day) €24 adult or €18 child, bullfight €18–€90.

Sightseeing. Admission prices for most museums are quite reasonable, on average €2–€4. Some places have no admission charge, and there are often student discounts and other concessions, including free entry to EU citizens on certain days.

Taxis. Taxis are generally inexpensive, with a typical city-centre ride costing around €4 on the meter. Be sure to agree the rate for long-distance journeys beforehand.

C

CAMPING *(camping)*

Spanish campsites are divided into categories, and rates and facilities vary accordingly. All sites, however, have drinking water, toilets and showers, electricity and basic first-aid facilities, and all are under surveillance night and day. Rates depend to a large extent on the facilities available. For a complete list of campsites, consult the *Guía de Campings*, available from the Spanish National Tourist Office *(see Tourist Information Offices on page 170)* and some local bookshops. Camping outside of official sites is fine, provided you obtain permission from the landowner. Many campsites have good beach locations but you are not allowed to pitch your tent on tourist beaches, in urban areas, or within 1 km (½ mile) of an official site.

CAR HIRE *(coches de alquiler*; see also DRIVING)

Hiring a car before you go can avoid any uncertainties and can be cheaper too. Auto Europe, <www.autoeurope.com>, is one of the largest organisations offering discount rates – especially if you require a car with an automatic transmission or specialist vehicles such as 4-wheel drives. Fly-drive deals with airline companies can be good value if you know in advance that you want to hire a car: all the big car-hire companies have discount deals with airlines. On the internet <easyCar.com> offers inexpensive deals.

Otherwise, you'll find a choice of car-hire firms in any major town, with the market leaders – Avis, Hertz, Europcar – at the airports and principal railway stations. Rates and conditions vary enormously. CDW insurance cover should be considered a necessity. Extra insurance cover against theft of radio and other car parts, and damage caused by thieves, is well worth considering.

Normally you must be over 21 to hire a car, and you will need a valid driver's licence that you have held for at least 12 months, your passport and a credit card – to use to leave a deposit. Visitors from countries other than the US, Canada and those in the EU will be expected to present an International Driver's Licence.

National local rate phone numbers: Avis 902 180 854; Hertz 917 499 069; Europcar 902 105 030.

I'd like to hire a car (tomorrow).	**Quisiera alquilar un coche (para mañana).**
for one day/a week	**por un día/una semana**
Please include full insurance.	**Haga el favor de incluir el seguro a todo riesgo.**

CLIMATE

As a general rule, late spring to early summer and late summer to early autumn are the best times for visiting most parts of Spain. This avoids the most oppressive heat, not to mention the crowds and high-season hotel rates. In winter, temperatures plummet in the high central plains. Summer temperatures in the north are ideal for swimming and sunbathing, but expect rain any time in the northwest. At the height of summer (July–August) even the locals try to escape the dry, merciless heat of Madrid and the central plains; the southern and east coast areas can be uncomfortably humid.

For winter sun, head for the Canary Islands where temperatures rarely fall below a monthly average of 17°C (62°F). On the mainland, the south coast and parts of the central and southeastern coast are pleasantly mild all year, but swimming is not really an option in winter. Of course, winter is the season for skiing in the Pyrenees, Picos de Europa and Andalucía's Sierra Nevada.

CLOTHING (ropa)

If you're heading for the south coast in the height of summer, pack loose cotton clothes and remember to take sun hats and sunscreen. In April, May and October, you may need a light sweater for the evenings. From November to March, you should enjoy shirt-sleeve sunshine during the day, but this can be interrupted by chill winds from the mountains, so take a warm jacket or sweater.

Winter visitors to Madrid and the central plains region will need to pack warm clothing. If you're heading for the northwest at any time, take waterproof gear.

Dress codes are very casual in most resorts, but tourists sporting resort wear in a big, sophisticated city such as Madrid or Barcelona may attract stares. The Spanish enjoy dressing up for an occasion, and it is as well to look smart if you are visiting a good restaurant or reputable nightclub. Short skirts, shorts and beachwear are considered inappropriate attire for visits to churches, so carry a wrap to cover bare arms and legs.

COMPLAINTS

By law, all hotels and restaurants must have official complaint forms (*hoja de reclamaciones*) and produce them on demand. The original of this triplicate document should be sent to the Ministry of Tourism; one copy remains with the establishment involved and one copy is given to you. The very action of asking for the *hoja* may resolve the problem in itself, as the establishment knows that tourism authorities take a serious view of such complaints.

I'd like to see the manager.	**Quiero ver al encargado.**

CRIME AND SAFETY

Spain's crime rate is on a par with the rest of Europe. Be on your guard against pickpockets and bag snatchers. Here are a few precautions. Always carry a minimum of cash and keep your passport, travellers' cheques, credit cards and cash in a money belt or, better still, in your hotel safe. Never leave bags unattended or out of reach, especially when swimming.

The most common crime against the tourist in Spain is theft from hire cars. If you park overnight in the street in one of the big towns or resorts, it's possible that your car will be broken into. Always look for secure parking areas. Lock your car and stow any possessions, especially video cameras and valuables, out of sight in the boot (trunk); never leave anything in your car overnight.

All thefts must be reported to the police within 24 hours. Go to the nearest police station (*comisaria*) and make a *denuncia*. You will need a copy of the police report in order to make a claim on your holiday insurance. As a precaution, photocopy the relevant pages of your passport(s) and airline ticket(s) and keep them in a separate place from the originals. This will save much time in the event of them being stolen. If this happens your consulate should also be informed *(see Embassies and Consulates on page 158)*.

I want to report a theft.	**Quiero denunciar un robo.**
My handbag/ticket/wallet/ passport has been stolen	**Me han robado el bolso/el billete/la cartera/el pasaporte.**
Help! Thief!	**¡Socorro! ¡Ladrón!**

CUSTOMS *(aduana)* AND ENTRY FORMALITIES

Most visitors, including citizens of EU countries, the US, Canada, Australia and New Zealand, require only a valid passport to enter Spain. Nationals of countries that do not have a reciprocal agreement with Spain need a visa. Visa requirements do change, so check the situation with the Spanish Embassy in your country before leaving.

Currency restrictions. Tourists may bring an unlimited amount of currency in any form into the country, although amounts over €6,000 must be declared.

I have nothing to declare.	**No tengo nada a declarar.**

D

DRIVING

As throughout Europe, in Spain you drive on the right, overtake on the left and, in the absence of road markings to the contrary, give way to traffic coming from the right. By law, drivers must have with them a valid driving licence, vehicle registration document and valid insurance documents issued by your insurance company, and must be able to show a passport or ID card.

Road conditions. Main roads and motorways (which are toll roads) are often very good and improving all the time, secondary roads less so.

Rules and regulations. Speed limits are 50km/h (30mph) in built-up areas, 90–100km/h (55–60mph) on main roads, and 120km/h (75mph) on motorways. The use of front and rear seat belts is obligatory. A red warning-triangle and set of spare bulbs must be carried and you should display a nationality sticker. You must have a yellow reflective jacket in the car (not in the boot) to be used in case of roadside emergency. Motorcycle riders and their passengers must wear crash helmets. Don't drink and drive: the permitted blood-alcohol level is low and penalties are stiff, and random breath tests are often carried out.

Spanish roads are patrolled by the motorcycle police of the Civil Guard *(Guardia Civil)*. They can impose on-the-spot fines for minor offences, including speeding, travelling too close to the car in front, and driving with deficient lights.

Fuel and oil service stations are plentiful, but keep an eye on the fuel gauge in more remote areas. Unleaded petrol *(gasolina sin plomo)* comes in two grades, super and super-plus, and diesel *(gasóleo)* is widely available.

Full tank, please, top grade.	**Llénelo, por favor, con super**.
Check the oil/tyres/battery.	**Por favor, controle el aceite/ los neumáticos/la batería**.

Parking (*aparcamiento*). Parking regulations are strictly enforced – offending vehicles will be towed away, and a hefty fine charged for their return. Some no parking signs have a large 'E' (*estacionamiento*) with a diagonal line through it. A yellow-painted kerb means parking is prohibited at all times. Blue means parking is restricted to certain times and that you have to pay for and display a sticker inside your window, usually obtained from a nearby machine (*expendedor de tickets de estacionamiento*). These spaces are for a maximum of two hours. Parking is usually free on Sundays and public holidays. Underground car parks with a security attendant are often the safest bet.

Road signs. Most of the road signs used in Spain are international pictograms. Here are some written signs you will come across:

Autopista (de peaje)	(Toll) motorway (expressway)
Ceda el paso	Give way (Yield)
Circunvalación	Bypass/ring-road
Curva peligrosa	Dangerous bend
Despacio	Slow
Desviación	Diversion (Detour)
Obras	Road works
Peligro	Danger
Prohibido aparcar	No parking
Salida de camiones	Lorry (Truck) exit

Breakdowns and assistance. For emergencies dial 112. On motorways there are SOS boxes located on both sides of the carriageway at 2km (1 mile) intervals.

My car has broken down. Where is the nearest garage?	**Mi coche se ha estropeado ¿Donde está el garage más cercano?**

E

ELECTRICITY *(corriente eléctrica)*

220V/50Hz AC is now standard. Sockets take round, two-pin plugs, so you may need an adapter.

EMBASSIES AND CONSULATES *(embajadas y consulados)*

All embassies (a selection of which are listed below) are in Madrid, and many countries have consular facilities in large cities, such as Barcelona and Sevilla, as well as in resort areas and islands popular with foreign tourists, such as the Costa del Sol, the Canary Islands and Palma, Mallorca. If you run into trouble with the authorities or the police, the embassy can advise you where to find the nearest consulate.

Australia Plaza Desc. Diego de Ordás 3, 2nd Floor, tel: 914 419 300.
Canada Núñez de Balboa 35, tel: 914 233 250.
Ireland Paseo de la Castellano 46, tel: 915 364 093.
South Africa Claudio Coello 91, tel: 914 363 780.
UK Fernando el Santo 16, tel: 913 700 8200.
US Serrano 75, tel: 915 872 200.

EMERGENCIES *(emergencias)*

Unless you are fluent in Spanish you should seek help through your hotel receptionist or the local tourist office. If you can speak Spanish, the following telephone numbers may be useful.

Ambulance	Police	Sea Rescue
061	091	900 202 202

112 will connect you to Fire, Police or Ambulance.

ETIQUETTE

The Spanish are still, by and large, an easy-going, friendly people, but politeness and simple courtesies still matter here. Always begin a conversation with *buenos días* (good morning), *buenas tardes* (good afternoon) or *buenas noches* (good evening), and sign off with *adiós* (goodbye) when leaving. And a handshake never goes amiss. One of the most enjoyable features of Spanish everyday life is unfortunately dying out: the evening *paseo* when young and old alike come out to take a stroll, see and be seen, and build up an appetite for supper.

When eating in a restaurant, you must always ask for the bill (*la cuenta*). It is very rarely offered, as no waiter wishes to be seen to be actually encouraging you to leave. Since a service charge is normally included in both hotel and restaurant bills, tipping is not obligatory, but if the service was good, you might leave 5–10 percent of the bill.

When sightseeing, dress respectfully for visits to churches, and don't forget the long midday break when planning your itinerary. Many museums and attractions, as well as shops and businesses, are firmly closed from around 1 or 2pm until 4 or 5pm.

Children are welcome just about anywhere you go in Spain – including bars and restaurants – and everyone likes to make a fuss of them.

G

GETTING THERE

By air from North America. Iberia, tel: 1 800 772-4642; <www. iberia.com> has flights from New York City and Miami to Madrid, and connections from there to Málaga, Sevilla and other smaller airports; Air Europa, tel: 1 800 238 7672, <www.air-europa.com>, has flights from New York City to Madrid, and connections from there to Málaga, Sevilla and other smaller airports. It also has a weekly scheduled flight between New York City and Málaga, in each direction. Spanair, tel: 1 888 545-5757, <www.spanair.com>, flies out of Washington DC and has flights to Madrid with onward connections to most destinations. Spanair also offers the economical Spain Pass, good for travel on the mainland and the Canary Islands.

By air from Europe. Scheduled flights link major European cities directly to the most important cities, and charter flights arrive in their hundreds from numerous destinations in northern Europe.

By car. From the UK, the main route from the French ferry ports runs south through western France to Bordeaux and into Spain at Irún, west of the Pyrenees. Alternatively, take the more central route through France to Perpignan in the southeast, then you can follow the A7 motorway to Barcelona and other points south.

Driving time can be cut by using the long-distance car-ferry service from Plymouth to Santander and Portsmouth to Bilbao in northern Spain *(see below)*.

By rail. From the UK, take the high-speed Eurostar (<www.eurostar.com>) from London's Waterloo International, through the Channel Tunnel to Paris. French National Railways, SNCF (<www.sncf.com>) operate high-speed TGV trains from either Gare Montparnasse or Gare d'Orleans in Paris to the French/Spanish border at Hendaye/Irún or Cerbere/Port Bou, on the western and eastern sides of the Pyrenees respectively. From either of those places change to a Spanish train (<www.renfe.es>) and head for your destination of choice.

By sea. From the UK, two companies offer car ferry services to mainland Spain, with schedules varying by the season. Brittany Ferries, tel: 08703 665 333, has sailings with an average crossing time of 24 hours between Plymouth and Santander and P&O European Ferries, tel: 0870 520 2020, has sailings with an average crossing time of 35 hours between Portsmouth and Bilbao.

GUIDES AND TOURS *(guías; visitas guidas)*

An English-speaking guide can be contacted through most local tourist offices. Tourist offices can also provide details of city walking tours and bus-tour operators in their area. They can assist with itineraries and may arrange bookings for you, possibly for a nominal fee. Guided tours and excursions can also be booked through your hotel reception desk in most resort areas and large cities, and through travel agencies *(agencia de viaje)*. Check at the time of booking that your guide will be able to speak your language.

H

HEALTH AND MEDICAL CARE

Anything other than basic emergency treatment can be very expensive, and you should not leave home without adequate insurance, preferably including cover for an emergency flight home in the event of serious injury or illness.

EU citizens are entitled to free emergency hospital treatment – in order to qualify you must obtain a European Health Insurance Card (EHIC) before you leave. For information, tel: 0845 606 2030; apply online at <www.dh.gov.uk> or obtain an application form from the post office. You may have to pay part of the price of treatment or medicines; keep receipts so that you can claim a refund when you return home.

One of the main health hazards is also Spain's biggest attraction – the sun. Take along a sun hat, sunglasses and plenty of sunscreen, and limit your sunbathing sessions to under an hour until you begin to tan. For minor ailments, visit the local first-aid post *(ambulatorio)*. Away from your hotel, don't hesitate to ask the police or a tourist information office for help. At your hotel, ask the staff for assistance. *Farmacias* (chemist/drugstore) are usually open during normal shopping hours, a green cross on a white background signifies a chemist.

After hours, at least one chemist per town remains open all night; called a *farmacia de guardia*, its location and emergency opening times are posted in the window of all other chemists and in the local newspapers.

Where's the nearest (all-night) chemist?	**¿Dónde está la farmacia (de guardia) más cercana?**
I need a doctor/dentist.	**Necesito un médico/dentista.**
sunburn/sunstroke	**quemadura del sol/una insolación**
an upset stomach	**dolor de estómago**

HOLIDAYS *(días festivos)*

Banks, post offices, government offices and many other businesses will be closed on the following national holidays. They may also shut on local and regional holidays; check with the local tourist office.

1 January	*Año Nuevo*	New Year's Day
6 January	*Epifanía*	Epiphany
March/April	*Jueves Santo*	Maundy Thursday
	Viernes Santo	Good Friday
1 May	*Día del Trabajo*	Labour Day/May Day
May/June	*Corpus Christi*	Corpus Christi
15 August	*Asunción*	Feast of the Assumption
12 October	*Día de la Hispanidad*	Columbus Day
1 November	*Todos los Santos*	All Saints' Day
6 December	*Día de la Constitución*	Constitution Day
8 December	*Immaculada Concepción*	Immaculate Conception
25 December	*Día de Navidad*	Christmas Day

L

LANGUAGE *(idoma; lenguaje)*

The national language of Spain, Castilian Spanish *(castellano)*, is spoken throughout the country. But it is estimated that two out of every five Spaniards speak another language primarily, and this trend has been especially marked since the decentralisation of some political powers to the regions. The inhabitants of the Basque Country, Galicia, Catalunya and the Balearics speak Euskara, Gallego, Catalan and variants of Catalan, respectively.

English is widely spoken in the resort towns, though it is polite to learn at least a few basic phrases. The Berlitz Spanish Phrasebook and Dictionary covers most situations you are likely to encounter, and the

Berlitz Spanish-English/English-Spanish pocket dictionary contains some 12,000 entries, plus a menu-reader supplement.

LOST PROPERTY *(objetos perdidos*; see also CRIME)

For items left behind on public transport, ask your hotel receptionist to telephone the bus or railway station or taxi company. If you still cannot find the missing item, then report the loss to the Municipal Police or the Guardia Civil within 24-hours *(see Police, page 165)*. They will issue a form that you will need if you wish to make an insurance claim once you are home.

M

MEDIA

Radio and television *(radio; televisión)*. Depending upon where you are it is possible, most especially on the Costas and in the Canary Islands and parts of the Balearics, to find radio stations that broadcast in English on the FM band. Network television programmes are all in Spanish, but better hotels and many English bars also have satellite TV with CNN, MTV, Superchannel, Sky TV, etc.

Newspapers and magazines *(periódico, revista)*. In the major tourist areas you can buy most European newspapers on the day of publication, with some English ones even having Spanish editions, but at about three times the price. The *International Herald Tribune* is also widely available, as are British and American magazines. In the Costas and the islands there are any number of weekly/monthly English language newspapers and magazines, some of which are free.

MONEY MATTERS

The monetary unit of Spain is the euro (€); with 100 cents making 1 euro. Banknotes are issued in denominations of 5, 10, 20, 50, 100, 200 and 500 euros. Coins in circulation are 1, 2, 5, 10, 20 and 50 cents. The euro is roughly equivalent to US$1.

Banks and currency exchange. Outside normal banking hours, many travel agencies and other businesses displaying a *cambio* sign will change foreign currency into euros. All larger hotels will also change guests' money. The exchange rate is slightly less favourable than at the bank. Traveller's cheques always get a better rate than cash. Always take your passport with you when you go to change money or traveller's cheques.

Cashpoints. ATMS outside banks are widely available in Spain, and are by far the easiest way of obtaining cash advances in euros, drawn on either your debit or credit card; they also provide a better exchange rate than cash or traveller's cheques. Check that your account and PIN number are authorised for international withdrawals.

Credit cards and travellers' cheques *(tarjetas de crédito; cheques de viajero)*. These are accepted in the majority of hotels, restaurants and big shops.

VAT (IVA). IVA *(impuesto sobre el valor agregado)*, value added tax, will be added to your hotel and restaurant bills; it currently stands at 7 percent. Generally these prices are included in the advertised total, though in some cafés and eating spots it is not, so best to peruse the menu carefully beforehand. In the Canary Islands value added tax is known as IGIC and levied at a rate of 4.5 percent on hotel rooms. If shops display a 'Tax Free Shopping' sign, then EU residents can get a refund on the tax if they make a big purchase.

Where's the nearest bank/ currency exchange office?	**¿Dónde está el banco/la casa de cambio más cercana?**
I want to change some pounds/dollars.	**Quiero cambiar libras/dólares**.
Do you take traveller's cheques?	**¿Acceptan cheques de viajero?**
Can I pay with a credit card?	**¿Se puede pagar con tarjeta?**
How much is that?	**¿Cuánto es/Cuánto vale?**

O

OPENING TIMES

Shops, offices and other businesses generally have a long lunch break, opening 9.30/10am to 1.30/2pm, and 4.30/5pm to 7.30/8pm, but in tourist areas many places now stay open all day. Museums, with few exceptions, also close at midday; many open for the morning only on Sunday, and most close all day on Monday. Banks generally open Monday to Friday 9am–2pm, and in winter on Saturday 9am–1pm, but beware of the numerous public holidays.

P

POLICE *(policía)*

There are three separate police forces in Spain. The Policía Municipal are attached to the local town hall and usually wear a blue uniform; they are the ones to whom you report theft and other crimes. The Policía Nacional is a national anti-crime unit whose officers wear a dark blue uniform; and the Guardia Civil, with green uniforms, is a national force whose most conspicuous role is to act as a highway patrol and customs officials. Spanish police, often working in pairs, are generally very courteous and helpful towards foreign visitors.

The emergency number is 112.

POST OFFICES *(correos)*

Post offices (<www.correos.es>) handle mail and telegrams only. You cannot normally make telephone calls from them. Opening hours vary slightly from town to town, but routine postal business is generally transacted Monday to Friday from 8.30am to 2.30pm, and on Saturday 9.30am to 1pm. All post offices are closed on Sunday. Postage stamps *(sellos)* are also on sale at tobacconists *(estancos)* and hotel desks, and at tourist shops selling postcards. Mail for destinations outside Spain should be posted in the box marked *extranjero* (overseas). Allow about a week for delivery to the US and 4–5 days to the UK. To speed things up, send a letter *urgente* (express) or *certificado* (registered).

PUBLIC TRANSPORT *(transporte publico)*

Buses *(autobús)*. These are cheap, reasonably comfortable and reliable in most areas, but beware of reduced timetables on Sundays. There are extensive bus services within and between major cities, but in the countryside services generally only run into and out of provincial centres – so links to smaller towns and resorts may not be possible, even if they are quite close by. Buses often go to destinations that are not served by trains, and are usually cheaper, faster and more frequent than trains.

Trains *(tren)*. Madrid is the hub of the RENFE (Spanish National Railways) network, which reaches out like a spider's web to most corners of the country. There is a bewildering number of different types of train service, from all-stops local services *(cercanias)* to the high-speed AVE that makes the trip from Madrid to Sevilla in just 2½ hours.

Timetables and information are available from railway stations and tourist offices, and from the RENFE website, <www.renfe.es>.

American visitors can take advantage of the Spain Flexipass, which gives three days of unlimited rail travel (in 1st or 2nd class) starting at US$175 (2nd class) or $225 (first class). Additional rail days are US$30 (2nd class) and US$35 (1st class) each. The Spain Rail 'n' Drive Pass gives three days of unlimited rail travel plus two days of car hire. Prices depend on class of rail travel and car category (four categories are available) and start at US$315 per person for two travelling together.

For information on further deals available, such as **Eurail** passes for UK visitors, and services including the high-speed Euromed (Barcelona, Valencia, Alicante) or AVE (Madrid, Córdoba, Sevilla, Cádiz, Málaga) trains, contact Rail Europe at <www.raileurope.com>. The website also contains useful rail trip planning information, especially the section on 'Fares and Schedules'.

Taxis *(taxi)*. In the major cities, taxis have meters, but in smaller towns and villages they usually don't, so it's a good idea to check the fare before you get in. If you take a long trip, you will be charged a two-way fare whether you make the return journey or not. By law a taxi may carry only four passengers. A green light and/or a *libre* (free) sign indicates a taxi that is available.

Ferries *(barcos)*. These are a useful form of transport between the Canary and Balearic islands themselves and, to a lesser extent, to and from the Canary Islands and the Balearics. Trasmediterránea (<www.trasmediterranea.com>) is the largest company operating ferry services in Spain.

Where is the (nearest) bus stop?	**¿Dónde está la parada de autobuses (más cercana)?**
When's the next bus/train for…?	**¿A qué hora sale el próximo autobús/tren para…?**
I want a ticket to…	**Quiero un billete para…**
single (one-way)	**ida**
return (round-trip)	**ida y vuelta**
Will you tell me when to get off?	**¿Podría indicarme cuándo tengo que bajar?**
How long does the journey take?	**¿Cuanto dura el viaje?**

R

RELIGION *(religión; servicios religiosos)*

The national religion is Roman Catholicism, and Mass is said regularly in churches great and small. In the main tourist centres, services are held in various languages. Most major cities have Protestant churches, mosques and synagogues, but services are held in Spanish unless there is a large resident English-speaking contingent in town – as there is on the Costa del Sol, for example.

T

TELEPHONE *(teléfonos)*

The country code for Spain is 34. All Spanish telephone numbers are 9-digit, and the number, which incorporates the area code, must be dialled in full – even for local calls.

There are phone booths in all major towns and cities from which you can make local and international calls. Instructions in English and dialling codes for different countries are displayed in the booths. Some telephones accept credit cards, and many require a phone card *(tarjeta telefónica)*, available from *tabacos*. To call abroad from Spain dial 00, then dial the country code, the area code (minus the initial 0) and the number. The country code for the US and Canada is 1; the UK 44; Australia 61; New Zealand 64; the Republic of Ireland 353; and South Africa 27.

Calling directly from your hotel room is almost always very expensive unless you use a calling card, or some other similar system, from your local long-distance supplier – in which case find out from the supplier the free connection number applicable to the countries; they are different for each country and these numbers are not always easily available once you are there.

Another economic option is to use a private booth that advertises its prices for particular countries in the window or on boards outside. Their rates are usually highly competitive, and you pay on completion of the call.

> Can you get me this number? **¿Puede comunicarme con este número?**

TIME ZONES

Spanish time is the same as that of most of Western Europe – Greenwich Mean Time plus one hour. In summer, another hour is added for

Daylight Saving Time (Summer Time), keeping it an hour ahead of British Summer Time. The time in the Canary Islands is one hour earlier than on mainland Spain.

New York	London	**Spain**	Sydney	Auckland
6am	11am	**noon**	8pm	10pm

TIPPING *(propina; servicio)*

Since a service charge is normally included on hotel and restaurant bills, tipping is not obligatory but it's usual to leave a small coin (about 5 percent of the bill) on a bar counter, and 5–10 percent on restaurant bills. If you tip taxi drivers, 5 percent is enough unless they are especially helpful. Additional guidelines:

Hotel porter, per bag	€0.50
Lavatory attendant	€0.30
Tour guide	10 percent
Hairdresser	10 percent
Taxi driver	5 percent
Maid, for extra services	€1

Is service (tip) included?	**¿Está incluído el servicio?**

TOILETS

The most commonly used expressions for toilets are *servicios* or *aseos*. Toilet doors are distinguished by *señoras* (ladies) or *damas* (women) and *caballeros* (men), and by pictograms.

Public conveniences are rare, but all hotels, bars and restaurants have toilets, usually of a reasonable standard, for the use of customers.

Where are the toilets?	**¿Dónde están los servicios?**

TOURIST INFORMATION OFFICES *(oficinas de información turística)*

There are Spanish National Tourist Offices in many countries. These include:

Canada 2 Bloor Street West, 34th Floor, Toronto, Ontario M4W 3E2, tel: (416) 961 3131, fax: (416) 961 1992, e-mail <toronto@tourspain.es>.

UK 22–3 Manchester Square, London, W1U 3PX, tel: (020) 7486 8077, fax: (020) 7486 8034, e-mail <londres@tourspain.es>.

US Water Tower Place, Suite 915 East, 845 N. Michigan Avenue, Chicago, IL 60611, tel: (312) 642 1992, fax: (312) 642 9817, e-mail <chicago@tourspain.es>.

8383 Wilshire Boulevard, Suite 960, Beverly Hills, Los Angeles, CA 90211, tel: (323) 658 7195, fax: (323) 658 1061, e-mail <losangeles@tourspain.es>.

666 Fifth Avenue, New York, NY 10103, tel: (212) 265 8822, fax: (212) 265 8864, e-mail <nuevayork@tourspain.es>.

1395 Brickell Avenue, Miami, FL 33131, tel: (305) 358 1992, fax: (305) 358 8223, e-mail <miami@tourspain.es>.

For further information check the website <www.spain.info>.

Where is the tourist office?   **¿Dónde está la oficina de turismo?**

TRAVELLERS WITH DISABILITIES

Facilities for travellers with disabilities are improving all the time, but as yet public transport is not wheelchair accessible. The Spanish National Tourist Office provides a fact sheet and a list of accessible accommodation. Many museums and other sights are not wheelchair accessible and a visit may require extensive walking.

Visually impaired travellers can contact ONCE, the Organización Nacional de Ciegos de España (Spanish National Organization for the Blind), Calle del Prado 24, 28041 Madrid, tel: 915 894 600.

W

WEBSITES

Spain's official tourism website is <www.spain.info>.
Regional websites are as follows:

Andalucía including Costa del Sol: <www.andalucia.org>

Aragón: <www.staragon.com>

Asturias: <www.infoasturias.com>

Balearic Islands: <www.illesbalears.es>

Barcelona: <www.barcelonaturisme.com>

Basque Country: <www.basquecountry-tourism.com>

Canary Islands: <www.grancanaria.com>, <www.webtenerife.com>, <www.cabildodelanzarote.com>

Cantabria: <www.turismo.cantabria.org>

Castilla La Mancha: <www.castillalamancha.es>

Castilla y León: <www.turismocastillayleon.com>

Catalonia: <www.catalunyaturisme.com>

Extremadura: <www.turismoextremadura.es>

Galicia: <www.turgalicia.es>

La Rioja: www.lariojaturismo.com

Madrid: <www.mundimadrid.es>

Murcia: <www.murcia-turismo.com>

Navarra: <www.navarra.es>

Valencia: <www.comunitatvalenciana.com>

Y

YOUTH HOSTELS *(albergues de juveniles)*

These are few and far between, but you can get a list from the YHA or the Spanish National Tourist Office. Many hostels operate in summer only, from temporary premises, so make sure you have an up-to-date list. An alternative is a *pensión* – these provide fairly basic rooms, some with three or four beds, and are often in town-centre locations.

Recommended Hotels

The following hotels and other types of accommodation in towns, cities and resorts throughout Spain are listed alphabetically. It is best to reserve well in advance, particularly if you will be visiting in the high season – which can vary from destination to destination and often coincides with important *fiestas*.

Prices do not normally include breakfast or IVA, the 7 percent value added tax. The symbols are an approximate guide to indicate the price for a double room with bath or shower in the high season. Low season rates can be considerably lower. It is sometimes possible to negotiate special deals or weekend rates

€€€€€	over 300 euros
€€€€	180–300 euros
€€€	120–180 euros
€€	90–120 euros
€	50–90 euros

ÁVILA

Hospedería La Sinagoga €/€€ *Reyes Católicos 22, tel: 920 352 321, fax: 920 353 474,<www.lasinagoga.com>*. In the 15th century this was one of Ávila's most important synagogues. Located in the heart of the city, it is now a modern small hotel where each room is different from the others. 22 rooms.

BARCELONA

Astoria €€€€ *París 203, tel: 932 098 311, fax: 932 023 008, <www.derbyhotels.es>*. A member of the Derby hotel chain, this is a sophisticated and quiet establishment a few paces from prime shopping territory on Diagonal. Built in the 1950s, the Astoria has been refurbished and is now very elegant. Some rooms have small sitting rooms or garden terraces. 117 rooms.

Condes de Barcelona €€€€ *Passeig de Gracia 73–75, tel: 934 450 000, fax: 934 453 232, <www. hotelcondesdebarcelona.com>.* Just a block away from Gaudí's La Pedrera, this popular hotel occupies two former palaces. The rooms are large, modern and elegant – ask for one with a Jacuzzi. A favourite of architects, designers, and European and Japanese tourists.109 rooms.

Gran Hotel Havana €€€€–€€€€€ *Gran Via de les Corts Catalanes 647, tel: 934 121 115, fax: 934 122 611, <www.granhotel havana.com>.* Founded in a charming house that dates from 1872, this was enlarged and renovated in 1991 into a deluxe hotel. It has an unusually shaped central atrium, around which are large, modern well-furnished rooms and suites, 24-hour room service. 145 rooms.

Mesón Castilla €€€ *Valldonzella 5, tel: 933 182 182, fax: 934 124 020, <www.mesoncastilla.com>.* A quiet, dignified hotel located on the Plaça Castilla just 100m or so from the Plaça Catulunya. Elegant public rooms and a private garage. 56 rooms.

Rivoli Ramblas €€€€ *La Rambla 128, tel: 933 026 643, fax: 933 175 053, <www.hotelriviliramblas.com>.* A busy town-house hotel on La Rambla, with the never-ending parade just beyond the front door. Smallish, well-equipped, sound-proofed rooms have a combination of art deco and avant-garde style. Great views from the terrace, where there is also a fitness centre, sauna and solarium. 130 rooms.

Sant Agustí €€ *Plaça Sant Agustí 3, tel: 933 181 658, fax: 933 172 928, <www.hotels.com>.* Supposedly the oldest hotel in the city, founded in 1840, in a pretty little square near La Rambla. 77 rooms.

BILBAO

López de Haro €€€–€€€€ *Obispo Orueta 2, tel: 944 235 500, fax: 944 234 500, <www.hotellopezdeharo.com>.* The top hotel in Bilbao, located in a renovated 19th-century structure, combines a classical style with every latest facility and has a fine restaurant. In the city centre and close to the Guggenheim Museum. 53 rooms.

CARMONA

Casa de Carmona €€€–€€€€ *Plaza de Lasso 1, tel: 954 191 000, fax: 954 190 189, <www.casadecarmona.com>.* A 16th-century palace lovingly renovated into a beautiful, hospitable, luxurious hotel. Every room is unique, and filled with handpicked antiques from Madrid, London and Paris. 34 rooms.

CÓRDOBA

NH Amistad Córdoba €€€ *Plaza Maimónides 3, tel: 957 420 335, fax: 957 420 365, <www.nh-hotels.com>.* Located in the Jewish quarter close to the Mezquita, two 18th-century mansions, next to the old Moorish wall, have been combined and restored to form a fully modernised hotel in harmony with this historic city. 84 rooms.

COSTA DEL SOL

Kempinski Resort Hotel €€€€€ *Carretera de Cádiz Km 159, Estepona, tel: 952 809 500, fax: 952 809 550, <www.kempinski-spain.com>.* All rooms in this architecturally interesting hotel (opened 1999) have a sea view. Guests enjoy a marvellous subtropical garden, a 1-km beach, several pools, watersports and horse-riding facilities, an haute-cuisine restaurant and the Polly Mar Thalasso Wellness centre. Puerto Banús is 10km (6 miles) west. 149 rooms.

Roc Lago Rojo €€ *Miami 1, La Carihuela, tel: 952 387 666, fax: 952 380 891, <www.roc-hotels.com>.* Just 2km (1 mile) from the centre of Torremolinos and 25m from La Carihuela beach, this is a charming modern hotel with good facilities. 144 rooms.

GRANADA

Alhambra Palace €€€ *Peña Partida 2, tel: 958 221 468, fax: 958 226 404, <www.h-alhambrapalace.es>.* Impressive Moorish-style palace on the edge of the hill on which stands the Alhambra (five minutes walk away), with stunning views across the city to the Sierra Nevada. 126 rooms.

Palacio de Santa Inés €€€ *Cuesta de Santa Inés 9, tel: 958 222 362, fax: 958 222 465, <www.palaciosantaines.com>.* The 16th-century palace known as the House of the Eternal Father has been beautifully converted into a hotel of considerable charm. It is located in the historic Albaicín area, on the opposite bank of the Darro from the towering Alhambra fortress. 35 rooms.

LEÓN

Parador de León €€€ *Plaza de San Marcos 7, tel: 987 237 300, fax: 987 233 458, <www.parador.es>.* Housed in an amazingly decorative 16th-century former convent, with an impressive Spanish Renaissance façade, this is one of Spain's finest and most luxurious *paradores*, as well as being a national monument. Ask for a room in the atmospheric old part, with its tapestry-lined walls. 226 rooms.

MADRID

Arosa €€€–€€€€ *Calle de la Salud 21, tel: 915 321 600, fax: 915 313 127, <www.hotelarosa.com>.* Centrally located, just off the Gran Vía and not far from the Puerta del Sol. Rooms range from the grand old style of the original building to sleek, modern quarters. Swimming pool. 134 rooms.

Hesperia Madrid €€€€€ *Paseo de la Castellana 57, tel: 912 108 800, fax: 912 108 899, <www.hesperia-madrid.com>.* A modern contemporary-style hotel, the first of its kind in Madrid. Expect to find distinguished rooms and public areas, exemplary service and fine restaurants. 171 rooms.

París €€ *Alcalá 2, tel: 915 216 496, fax: 915 310 188.* Very central location, with a wonderful façade overlooking the Puerta del Sol. Traditional style and ambiance. 114 rooms.

Santo Domingo €€€–€€€€ *Plaza de Santa Domingo 13, tel: 915 479 800, fax: 915 475 995, <www.hotelsantodomingo.com>.* In a quiet location not far from the Puerta del Sol. Each room is different in style and décor from the others. 120 rooms.

Wellington €€€€€ *Velázquez 8, tel: 915 754 400, fax: 915 764 164, <www.hotel-wellington.com>*. A stylish hotel in a distinguished location close to the Prado and the Puerta de Alcála. All rooms have a classical décor combined with the latest in facilities. Fine restaurant and nice bar, too. 275 rooms.

MÉRIDA

Parador de Mérida €€€ *Plaza de la Constitución 3, tel: 924 313 800, fax: 924 319 208, <www.parador.es>*. Located in what was once an 18th-century convent that, itself, was on the site of a Roman Praetorian Guard palace. An elegant mix of history and style. 82 rooms.

PAMPLONA

Avenida €€€–€€€€ *Avenida de Zaragoza 5, tel: 948 245 454, fax: 948 232 323, <www.hotelavenida.biz>*. Has an unusual wedge-shaped façade, and the balconies of this restored building overlook the fountain on Plaza Príncipe de Viana. As usual in Pamplona, the rooms, although pleasant and comfortable, are not large. Prices increase significantly for two weeks in July during San Fermin. 24 rooms.

SALAMANCA

Rector €€–€€€ *Paseo del Rector Esperabe 10, tel: 923 218 482, fax: 923 214 008*. This magnificent building, once home to one of Salamanca's most aristocratic families, has been tastefully converted into a delightful small hotel. 13 rooms.

SAN SEBASTIÁN

La Galería €€€ *Infanta Cristina 1–3, tel: 943 216 077, fax: 943 211 298, www.hotellagaleria.com*. Handsome French-style 1890s house with individually decorated rooms. Situated not far from Ondarreta beach and the Palacio de Miramar, and close to San Sebastián's shops and *tapas* bars. 23 rooms.

María Cristina €€€€–€€€€€ *Calle Oquendo 1, tel: 943 437 676, fax: 943 437 600, <www.starwoodhotels.com>*. A grand belle-époque building dating from 1912 that used to be King Alfonso XIII's winter headquarters. A renovation in 1987 added modern facilities and extra luxuries to what is the finest hotel in San Sebastián. 139 rooms.

SANTIAGO DE COMPOSTELA

Hostal Dos Reis Católicos €€€€ *Plaza do Obradoiro 1, tel: 981 582 200, fax: 981 563 094, <www.parador.es>*. Built by the Catholic Monarchs in the late 15th century, and expanded in the 17th and 18th centuries, this is Spain's most famous *parador* and reputedly the world's oldest hotel. Located on a magnificent square, the *parador* combines history with modern facilities. 136 rooms.

SEGOVIA

Los Linajes €€ *Dr Velasco 9, tel: 921 460 475, fax: 921 460 479, <www.loslinajes.com>*. Just a two-minute walk from the Plaza Mayor, the hotel occupies a 17th-century building located on the edge of the old city, overlooking the countryside. Most rooms have a terrace. 55 rooms.

SEVILLA

Alfonso XIII €€€€€ *San Fernando 2, tel: 954 917 000, fax: 954 917 099, <www.hotel-alfonsoxiii.com>*. Opened by King Alfonso XIII in 1929, this imposing hotel in the city centre is set in its own lovely gardens and epitomises Sevillian style and luxury. The spacious rooms are classically decorated and the lobby bar is a meeting point for Sevilla's high society. 147 rooms.

Doña Maria €€€ *Don Remondo 19, tel: 954 224 990, fax: 954 219 546, <www.hdmaria.com>*. A charming hotel with an interesting mix of antiques and modern facilities and a rooftop pool and bar. Excellent central location, almost within touching distance of the Giralda and cathedral. 70 rooms.

Los Seises €€€€ *Segovias 6, tel: 954 229 495, fax 954 224 334, <www.hotellosseises.com>*. A 16th-century palace where historic surroundings combine with modern facilities to create an intriguing ambiance. Located in the Barrio de Santa Cruz, it has a rooftop pool overlooking the nearby cathedral and Giralda. 43 rooms.

Simón €€ *García de Vinuesa 19, tel: 954 226 660, fax: 954 562 241, <www.hotelsimonsevilla.com>*. A handsome hotel in a renovated 18th-century townhouse, across from the cathedral. 31 rooms.

TOLEDO

Parador de Toledo €€€ *Cerro del Emperador s/n, tel: 925 221 850, fax: 925 225 166, <www.parador.es>*. Comfortable rooms, a fine restaurant, traditional service and a pool – plus magnificent views over Toledo. 77 rooms.

Pintor El Greco €€ *Alamillos del Tránsito 13, tel: 925 285 191, fax: 925 215 819, <www.hotelpintorelgreco.com>*. Delightful 17th-century house, with pleasant rooms, modern comforts and car parking, located in a charming section of the old Jewish quarter close to most monuments. 33 rooms.

VALENCIA

Sidi Saler €€€€ *Playa del Saler, tel: 961 610 411, fax: 961 610 838, <www.sidisaler.com>*. This is as good as it gets: a wonderful hotel right on the Mediterranean, with a fine restaurant and health spa, and a free bus into Valencia, 15 minutes away. 276 rooms.

THE BALEARIC ISLANDS

IBIZA

Club Cala Moli €/€€ *Apartado 105, San Josep, tel: 971 806 002, fax: 971 806 150, <www.calamoli.com>*. Located in the quieter southeastern part of the island, this is a charming *hostal* with attractive views from the pool and patio out over the Mediterranean. 10 rooms.

Ca'spla €€€ *San Miguel de Balanzat, tel: 971 334 587, fax: 971 334 604, <www.caspla-ibiza.com>*. Listed as a 'Hotel Rural' this is at least as good as any 5-star hotel. Large and eclectically decorated rooms (some even with a private pool) are set in luxuriant grounds with wooden-beamed patios overlooking the pool. 16 rooms.

Hacienda Na Xamena €€€€/€€€€€ *San Miguel de Balanzat, tel: 971 334 500, fax: 971 334 514, <www.hotelhacienda-ibiza.com>*. Perched dramatically on high cliffs, overlooking the Mediterranean, this luxury hotel has the finest location on Ibiza. The décor is an intriguing mix of traditional Ibicenco style and art deco. 65 rooms.

MALLORCA

Convent de la Missió €€€ *Carrer de la Missió 7, Palma de Mallorca, tel: 971 227 347, fax: 971 227 348, <www.conventde-lamissio.com>*. This new stylish hotel, in a converted 17th-century convent in the old quarter, has light, airy rooms, a roof terrace, sauna and an excellent restaurant. There is an art gallery in the refectory. 14 rooms.

Es Molí €€€€€ *Carretera Valldemossa-Deià s/n, Deià, tel: 971 639 000, fax: 971 639 333, <www.hotelesmoli.com>*. An elegant hotel in a converted 19th-century manor house on a hill just outside Deià, with incomparable views of the village and the sea. The pool is spring-fed, and the hotel is set in 15,000 sq m (18,000 sq yd) of gardens. The service is splendid. Breakfast on the terrace. The highly recommended restaurant, Ca'n Quet, has its own garden. Closed November to mid-April. 87 rooms.

Formentor €€€€/€€€€€ *Playa de Formentor, tel: 971 899 101, fax: 971 865 155, <www.hotelformentor.net>*. In a fantastic location, possibly the best in the Balearics, surrounded by forests and with sculpted gardens leading onto a beautiful bay surrounded by mountains. A classical, formal hotel often frequented by famous personalities. Three restaurants and a health and beauty centre. 250 rooms.

MENORCA

Port Mahón €€€/€€€€ *Avenida Fort de l'Eau 13, tel: 971 362 600, fax: 971 351 050.* A charming hotel with an attractive façade, and gardens with a pool, overlooking the wide expanse of the well-protected Mahón harbour. Good size rooms, especially those with balconies overlooking the water. Swimming pool. 82 rooms.

Hostal Biniali €€ *Carretera S'Uestra-Binibeca 50, Sant Lluis, tel: 971 151 724, fax 971 150 352, <www.hostalbiniali.com>.* Set in it's own beautiful lawned gardens and surrounded by Menorcan countryside, this relaxed and friendly *hostal* is just 5 minutes from the sandy beaches of the south coast. 9 rooms.

THE CANARY ISLANDS

FUERTEVENTURA

Riu Palace Tres Islas €€/€€€ *Grandes Playas, Corralejo, tel: 928 535 700, fax: 928 535 858,<www.riu.com>.* Perfectly located on the magnificent beach, with a view of the dunes and Lanzarote. Very well appointed rooms, attractive pool and terrace, boutiques and nightly entertainment in the piano bar and Betancuria lounge. 365 rooms.

GRAN CANARIA

Club de Mar €/€€ *Urbanización Puerto de Mogán s/n, Playa de Mogán, tel: 928 565 066, fax: 928 565 438, <www.clubdemar. com>.* Enjoys a wonderful location at the end of the harbour in this delightful marina. Pleasant rooms with all the expected facilities, plus pool and bar and swimming in the harbour. 56 rooms.

Las Calas €€ *El Arenal, 36 La Lechuza, Vega de San Mateo, tel: 928 661 436, fax: 928 660 753, <www.hotelrurallascalas.com>.* A friendly old farmhouse converted into a small, relaxed boutique hotel high in the Gran Canaria countryside. Typical home-cooked Canarian food is served in the intimate dining room. 7 rooms.

LA GOMERA

Jardín Tecina €€€/€€€€ *Lomada de Tecina, Playa de Santiago, tel: 922 145 850, fax: 922 145 851, <www.jardin-tecina.com>*. A stylish complex set in its own extensive gardens on the cliffs. The hotel has an array of restaurants, bars, pools, sports facilities and it's own beach club. 434 rooms.

LA PALMA

Parador de la Palma €€€ *El Zumacal, Breña Baja, tel: 922 435 828, fax: 922 435 999, <www.parador.es>*. A *parador* located on the cliffs just to the south of, and overlooking, Santa Cruz. Traditionally Canarian in style and décor. 78 rooms.

LANZAROTE

Gran Meliá Salinas €€€€€ *Avenida Islas Canarias, Costa Teguise, tel: 928 590 040, fax: 928 590 390, <www.solmelia.es>*. The island's largest and most luxurious hotel, and an integral part of the cultural heritage of Lanzarote. The stunning double atrium is filled with magnificent indoor gardens and waterfalls – the creations, as is the pool, of César Manrique. 309 rooms.

TENERIFE

Bahia del Duque €€€€€ *Carretera Alcalde Walter Paetzmann, Playa de las Americas, Costa Adeje, tel: 922 713 000, fax: 922 746 925, <www.bahia-duque.com>*. An eclectic array of buildings set around a sub-tropical garden with pools, restaurants and bars that descend, over several levels, down to the beach. Traditionally dressed staff and peacocks roaming free. 362 rooms.

San Roque €€€ *Carretera Esteban de Ponte 32, Garachico, tel: 922 133 435, fax: 922 133 406, <www.hotelsanroque.com>*. A beguiling and eclectic mix of a traditional 17th-century palace with wooden beamed ceilings and balconies and modern art deco. The pool is set in a charming patio. 20 rooms.

Recommended Restaurants

Remember that local people eat lunch and dinner late *(see page 140)*. You can either join them in eating early-evening *tapas*, to stave off hunger pangs, or go just after the restaurants have opened, when foreign visitors are likely to be the only diners. Many restaurants offer a *menú del día*, particularly at lunchtime. This bargain fixed-price menu is in addition to their à-la-carte selections. Reservations are recommended for the more expensive places.

The following symbols give some idea of the average cost of a meal for two, excluding drinks.

€€€€	over 70 euros
€€€	50–70 euros
€€	25–50 euros
€	under 25 euros

ÁVILA

Doña Guiomar €€€ *Tomás Luís de Victoria 3, tel: 920 253 709.* Located in a beautifully restored building, this restaurant combines traditional style with classic and modern influences to create temptingly delicious dishes.

BARCELONA

Botafumeiro €€€€ *Gran de Gràcia 81, tel: 932 184 230.* Open daily for lunch and dinner. The city's top seafood restaurant is big and informal with plenty of action. The perfectly prepared and presented fish and shellfish dishes combine the best elements of Galician and Catalan cuisines. Great *tapas*: to get a seat at the seafood bar, go off-peak (noon–1pm, 7–8pm).

La Fonda Escudellers €€ *Carrer dels Escudellers 10, tel: 933 017 575.* This modern restaurant set on two levels is immensely popular especially at lunchtimes, as the queues outside testify. It is worth the wait for very good food at very reasonable prices.

Quo Vadis €€€€ *Carme 7, tel: 933 024 072*. A long-time favourite of Barceloneses, especially opera-goers (the Liceu Opera House is only a couple of minutes away). There are several small and casually elegant dining rooms. Open Monday to Saturday for lunch and dinner.

CÓRDOBA

El Churrasco €€€ *Romero 16, tel: 957 290 819*. Located in a 14th-century house in the Jewish quarter, with various dining areas each uniquely decorated. The seasonal cuisine is based on natural products, with wines from its own Museo del Vino (Wine Museum). Closed August.

COSTA DEL SOL

Taberna del Alabardero Club de Playa €€€ *Club de Playa Castiglione, San Pedro de Alcantara, tel: 952 785 138*. A beach restaurant specialising in *paellas* and fried fish. There is a gourmet branch of the Taberna del Alabardero not far away, on the road to Ronda *(tel: 952 812 794)*.

GRANADA

Sevilla €€€ *Oficios 12, tel: 958 221 223*. Granada's most famous restaurant was also once a favourite of García Lorca, the poet and dramatist. The menu offers a good mixture of local Granadino and Andalucían specialities. Closed Sunday evening.

MADRID

Casa Santa Cruz €€€/€€€€ *La Bolsa 12, tel: 915 218 623*. Probably the most beautiful and unusual restaurant in Madrid. The 15th-century building was once a chapel of the Santa Cruz church, later serving as the Stock Exchange. The top quality menu features dishes prepared using traditional Castilian recipes.

Lhardy €€€€ *San Jerónimo 8, tel: 915 222 207.* At first glance this looks like a very elegant and old-fashioned delicatessen. Founded in 1839, that is exactly what it is downstairs, but upstairs is a suite of elegant dining rooms, where you can expect a traditional gastronomic treat, whatever you decide to select from the menu.

Taberna del Alabardero €€€ *Felipe V 6, tel: 915 472 577.* Located close to the Royal Palace, it acquired the name Guardia de Alabarderos tavern, because it was a popular watering hole for the guards who used to march by on duty and later return for a drink. Now a fine restaurant serving excellent Basque food at remarkably good value – especially the *menú del día*.

Taberna Carmencita €€/€€€ *Calle Libertad 16, tel: 915 316 612.* Once the haunt of artists, soldiers and bullfighters, this rambling inn has been around since 1850. The original hand-painted tiles and the check tablecloths create a homely ambiance, appropriate to the Madrileño cooking. Croquettes, stuffed peppers, fillet steak, tripe, meatballs, eggs and the hotpot known as *cocido* are the mainstays.

PAMPLONA

Josetxo €€€€ *Plaza Príncipe de Viana 1, tel: 948 222 097.* Widely regarded as the city's finest and grandest restaurant. The specialities vary with the seasons and will include fresh fish dishes and frozen dessert truffles. Closed Sunday (except during San Fermín) and August.

SALAMANCA

Chapeau €€€ *España 20, tel: 923 265 795.* Considered one of the city's best restaurants, the Chapeau has a traditional ambiance. Dishes on La Creatividad menu can be ordered as main courses or in smaller portions that can be combined to form a *degustación* menu. Another menu specialises in local regional dishes. Reservations recommended.

SAN SEBASTIÁN

Arzak €€€€ *Alto de Miracruz 21, tel: 943 278 465.* This Michelin three-star restaurant specialises in traditional Basque cuisine. The superbly prepared game and seafood dishes are accompanied by a selection of classic wines. Closed Sunday evening, Monday (and Tuesday January–June) and two weeks in June and November.

SANTIAGO DE COMPOSTELA

A Barrola €€/€€€ *Rua Franco 29, tel: 981 577 999.* Passers-by are tempted in by a sumptuous window display of fish and shellfish. The house speciality is a shellfish combination, designed to be shared by two. The octopus in garlic with mussels is equally delicious.

SEGOVIA

José María €€€ *Cronista Lecea 11, tel: 921 461 111.* A firm favourite in Segovia, José María serves traditional Castilian fare with fine local wines in a lively, rustic ambiance. It is hard not to over-indulge in the wide selection of *tapas* on show in the bar.

SEVILLA

Egaña Oriza €€€ *San Fernando 41, tel: 954 227 211.* A renowned restaurant located in a beautiful building just across from Sevilla's old Tobacco Factory (the setting for Bizet's opera *Carmen*). The Egaña Oriza is famous for Jose María Egaña's dishes, which combine Basque influences with Andalucían traditions. The wine list features Spanish and international vintages. Closed Saturday lunchtime, Sunday and August.

Marea Grande €€€ *Diego Angulo Iñigiuez 16, tel: 954 538 000.* Just outside the city centre, this has a delightful ambiance and décor and offers an amazing array of seafood, with a fine wine list and excellent service.

TOLEDO

Casón de los López de Toledo €€€ *Sillería 3, tel: 925 254 774.* Located in an impressive historic building just off the Plaza de Zocodover, this fine restaurant has three separate dining rooms (Christian Room, Corpus Room and Arab Room), each with its own distinctive style. Very informative wine list. Closed Monday night and Tuesday.

VALENCIA

Rías Gallega €€€ *Cirilo Amorós 4, tel: 963 512 125.* Established for over 30 years, this restaurant specialises in Galician cuisine. Unusually, many of the dishes can be ordered in half portions. Closed Sunday and August.

THE BALEARIC ISLANDS

IBIZA

Restaurante del Carmen € *Platja Cala D'Hort, tel: 971 187 449.* What this restaurant lacks in haute-cuisine and style it more than makes up for in location. It overlooks the quiet beach and has, arguably, the best views of the mystic Es Vedra rock.

Sueno de Estrellas €€€€ *San Miguel, tel: 971 334 500.* The delightful gourmet restaurant of the Hotel Hacienda Na Xamena is set on two levels overlooking the pool and cliffs. Whether you select the daily menu, the special seven-course menu or à la carte, expect delightfully thought-out and well-presented dishes.

MALLORCA

Koldo Royo €€€/€€€€ *Ingeniero Gabriel Roca 3, Palma de Mallorca, tel: 971 732 435.* On the Passeig Marítím, overlooking the harbour, this is a fine restaurant indeed. Koldo Royo trained in San Sebastian, and that shows in his imaginative Basque recipes. Expect delightfully presented dishes such as 'warm and cold cream of green peas and asparagus soup', drunk from a glass. Closed Sunday evening and second half of November.

El Olivo €€€€ *Son Canals, Deià, tel: 971 639 011*. One of the island's top restaurants, part of La Residencia Hotel. Delicious nouvelle cuisine. Try the gastronomic menu if you feel flush. The terrace dining is difficult to top for sheer romance. Dinner only. Closed Monday and Tuesday.

El Pi €€€€ *Formentor, tel: 971 899 100*. This is the gourmet restaurant of the Hotel Formentor. With the pool and Mediterranean as a backdrop, enjoy classical Mallorcan cuisine. Dinner only.

Ses Porxeres €€€ *Carretera Palma-Soller, Km17, Bunyola, tel: 971 613 762*. A beautiful Catalan restaurant near the Jardins d'Àlfabia. Specialities include game, fish stews and lamb cutlets grilled on hot rocks at your table. Reservations essential, especially for Sunday lunch. Closed Sunday evening, Monday and August.

Ses Rotjes €€€–€€€€ Carrer Rafael Blanes 21, Cala Ratjada, tel: 971 563 108. This restaurant, in the hotel of the same name, has a Michelin star and is a delightful find. Although fresh fish is their speciality, they don't neglect the meat dishes. An extensive wine list. Reservations advisable. Closed mid-November to mid-March.

MENORCA

Es Plá €€€€ *Pasaje Es Plá, Fornells, tel: 971 376 655*. The island's most famous restaurant, patronised by King Juan Carlos, who comes here for the *caldereta de langosta*, a delicious lobster stew. There are plenty of other good things to try.

THE CANARY ISLANDS

GRAN CANARIA

Amaiur €€€ *Calle Pérez Galdós 2, Las Palmas, tel: 928 370 717*. Beautifully presented dishes from the Basque country in a restaurant run by a man who knows and loves good food. Small, sweet peppers filled with *bacalao* are among the specialities. Closed Sunday.

LA GOMERA

Club Laurel €€€€ *Lomada de Tecina, 38810 Playa de Santiago, tel: 922 145 850.* The à la carte restaurant of the Jardín Tecina resort is located by the beach, and is reached by means of a lift that passes through the cliff. The great location is combined with a romantic ambiance, live guitar music, haute cuisine and fine wines, making it a perfect choice for a romantic night out. Evenings only, closed Sunday. Reservations essential.

LA PALMA

Restaurante La Placeta €€€ *Placeta Borrero 1, tel: 922 415 273.* Located in a charming old house, this restaurant has a delightful ambiance. Wooden floors, beams, staircase and old windows are the setting for home-cooked international-style cuisine with an emphasis on fish, meats and sauces. Open daily 7–11pm.

LANZAROTE

La Era €€€€ *El Barranco 3, Yaiza, tel: 928 830 016.* Set in a charming 300-year-old typical Canarian country house, with a whitewashed patio courtyard decked with flowers, La Era serves outstanding island specialities. There is also an art-filled wood-beamed bar that serves snacks and light meals, and a craft shop. The décor owes much to César Manrique's artistic creations. Closed Monday.

TENERIFE

El Duende €€€ *La Higuerita 41 Puerto de la Cruz, tel: 922 374 517.* One of the most highly commended restaurants in the old holiday resort of Puerto de la Cruz on the north of the island. Excellent menu. Closed Monday and Tuesday, and lunchtime Wednesday and Thursday.

INDEX